I0045363

EXPORT AND IMPORT
DOCUMENTATION AND PROCEDURES

EXPORT AND IMPORT DOCUMENTATION AND PROCEDURES

Dr. J. Senthilvelmurugan, MBA, M.com,,PGDCA, Ph.D.,
Periyar Institute of Management Studies (PRIMS),
Periyar University
Salem-11

S. Mahalakshmi, MBA, MCS, M.Phil, Ph.D.,
Dept.of Management Studies
Mahendra Arts & Science College,
Namakkal (Dt).

MJP Publishers

Chennai   New Delhi   Tirunelveli

ISBN 978-81-8094-183-2

Printed and bound in India

© K. Senthilvelmurugan
S.Mahalakshmi

MJP 164

MJP Publishers

New No. 5 Muthu Kalathy Street,

Triplicane,

Chennai 600 005

2013

This book has been published in good faith that the work of the author is original. All efforts have been taken to make the material error-free. However, the author and publisher disclaim responsibility for any inadvertent errors.

PREFACE

Documentation procedures have become an essential part of trade. The export and import documentation procedures have gained much importance with the countries expanding their trade as a result of reduced barriers. Many Indian Universities have incorporated the subject, Export–Import trade and their procedures in their curricula on account of its gaining importance.

This book has been prepared keeping in mind the needs of the students studying BBA, BBM, B.Com CA, M.B.A and such similar courses offered by the Universities of Periyar, Bharathiar, Annamalai, and other Universities.

This book is suitable for both Regular and correspondence students. This book caters the need of both students and staff members in simple language.

Previous years question papers have been incorporated to enable the students to prepare for their examination.

Suggestions for the improvements of this book are welcome.

Dr. J. Senthilvelmurugan
S. Mahalakshmi

CONTENTS

Chapter -I

1.1 IMPORT EXPORT DOCUMENTATION AND FRAMEWORK

INTRODUCTION:

Exporting is a trading process, where goods are sold in the foreign market. Since independence, India had a classed economy which led to the difficulties in paying the foreign currencies. After the liberalization in 1991, the entire trade of the country has seen an enormous improvement. Moreover, it is necessary for a Country to export in order to have foreign currency without which the imports cannot be done.

A developing country like India cannot import materials, technology required for development, equipments, tools and spares etc. There prevails an exchange system wherein the surpluses are exported and deficits are imported. When the inflow of money into a country is excess than the outflow, there is surplus of balance of payments. On the contrary, when there is outflow is more than the inflow, there is a deficit in balance of payments. This balance of payment is a statement of accounts that shows the difference between the amounts of money that has flown into and out of the country, within a particular period a time.

Export means selling the home country's goods/services in a foreign country. If goods made in India are sold in US, then those goods are exported to US. Imports are just the opposite of exports. Here, goods/services are purchased and brought in from another country.

India has seen a great growth in exports and imports after 1991* due to the liberalization of the economy. All the major sectors of the economy have seen policy changes leading to positive steps toward globalization. As a result, we have an increasing number of international companies coming to India. Likewise, Indian companies have also expanded abroad, and continue to do so. Wipro, Reliance Infosys, TCS, Ranbaxy, the Aditya Birla Group are best examples of Indian companies' international efforts.

MEANING OF EXPORT MARKETING:

Export marketing is the first step and international marketing. Exports mean selling of goods/services to another country. However, the following conditions are essential for an export transaction.

This is shown in the following diagram:

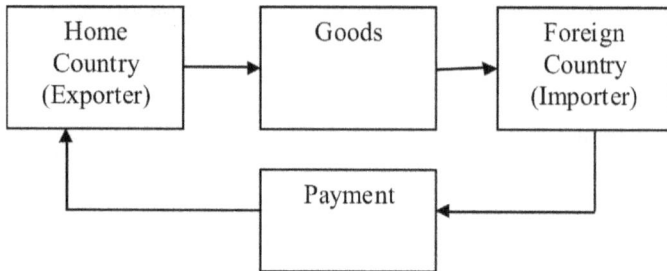

```
┌─────────────┐        ┌─────────┐        ┌─────────────┐
│   Home      │        │  Goods  │        │  Foreign    │
│  Country    │───────▶│         │───────▶│  Country    │
│ (Exporter)  │        │         │        │ (Importer)  │
└─────────────┘        └─────────┘        └─────────────┘
       ▲                                         │
       │               ┌─────────┐               │
       └───────────────│ Payment │◀──────────────┘
                       │         │
                       └─────────┘
```

- Goods/services must be sent across the national border to another country.
- Payment for the goods must be realised in the exporter's country.

This is shown in the following diagram:

The home country in this case is the country of the exporter (seller) and the foreign country is the country of the importer (buyer). The goods have to physically move to the foreign country and the payment for the same has to be realized in the home country.

Similarly, an import transaction involves buying and physically transporting goods from a foreign country into one's home country and despatching payment for the same to the foreign country.

Exports are a vital part of any economy. These result in efficient allocation of resources, better capacity utilization, exploitation of economics of scale and technological improvement, as a result of competition in foreign markets.

1.2 ADVANTAGES FOR THE HOME COUNTRY:

Exports	Imports
Foreign exchange earnings	Foreign Exchange outlay
Better profits	Makes available scarce/Unavailable inputs
Improved quality	Technical know-how
Access to new markets	Aid to exports
Capacity utilization	Better relations

Exporting is the most traditional and safe way of entering into a foreign market. It involves marketing of goods produced in the domestic country in another country. It does not involve any manufacturing in the foreign country.

India's share in the global trade has increased from 0.4% in 1980-95 to 1.1 percent in 2004 to 1.5 percent in 2006 and will cross the two percent in 2009. Foreign trade, as a percentage of GDP (in rupee terms) was over 25% in 2006, up from 14.1 percent in 1990-91. India's share in world trade has doubled from 0.4% in 1991 to 0.8% in 2003 to 1.5% in 2006 to 2% on 2009.

Exports:

India's chief exports include computer software, agricultural products (cashews, coffee), cotton textiles and clothing (ready-made garments, cotton yarn and textiles), gems and jewellery, cut diamonds, handicrafts, iron ore, jute products, leather goods, shrimp, tea, and tobacco. The country also exports industrial goods, such as appliances, electronic products, transport equipment, light machinery as well as chemical and engineering products. India imports rough diamonds, cuts them, and exports the finished gems. India's main exports in 2005 included USA 16.7%, UAE 8.5%, China 6.6%, Singapore 5.3%, UK 4.9%, and Hong Kong 4.4%. India's services contributed about 35% of the total exports as of 2010-11.

Total Exports by India:

1997-98	2002-03	2005-06	2010-11
Rs 130,101 Cr.	Rs.250,130 Cr.	Rs.454,800 Cr.	Rs.9,00,471 Cr
Source: Indian Ministry of Commerce and Industry.			

Imports:

Capital goods and fuel, each account for about a quarter of Indian imports. Other imports of India include edible oils, fertilizer, food grains, iron and steel, industrial machinery, professional instruments and transportation equipment. Chemicals, precious and semi-precious stones and non-ferrous metals are the other major imports. India's main import partners included China 7.3%, US 5.6%, Switzerland 4.7%.

1997-98	2002-03	2005-06	2007-08
Rs 154,176 Cr.	Rs. 297,206 Cr.	Rs. 630,527 Cr.	Rs. 949,133 Cr.
Source: Indian Ministry of Commerce and Industry			

Deficits:

The value of India's imports is greater than the value of its exports. India uses foreign loans to finance the extra imports. With exports and earnings on the invisibles account improving, the trade deficit in 2000/01 narrowed to $5.73 billion from $12.9 billion in the year-ago period. Current account deficit was about US$ 3.7 billion or about 1.4 percent of GDP in 1996-97, down from 3.2 percent in 1990-91.

1.3   TYPES OF EXPORTERS:

Exporters are divided as following categories:

- **Active and passive.** Active exporters are the ones who work hard on marketing their products to buyers abroad through various channels. In fact, they spend considerable time and money in their marketing efforts. On the other hand, a passive exporter is only a reactor and he waits for the opportunity to receive an export order and works only upon producing that order. He does not spend either time or money for marketing abroad.

- **Manufacturer exporters and Merchant exporters:** Exporters could be classified as manufacturer exporters and Merchant exporters.

An exporter who does manufacturing himself is called a Manufacturer exporter and an exporter who buys products from another source and then exports them is called a Merchant exporter.

- **Service and Project Exporters:** The export of Services to other countries is called service exports. Example Software consultancy services, technical and professional services like engineering, legal and financial services, Project exports involve executing a specific work-plan in a foreign country within a specific time frame. Examples of project exports are setting up of factories and power plants, and construction of dams, flyovers and building complexes.

- **Direct and Indirect Exporters:** Export can be of direct or indirect nature. In direct exporting, the organization generally uses an agent, distributor, or acts through a government agency. Indirect methods of exporting means using export management companies and trading companies.

- In Direct exports they sell or supply goods/services to buyers abroad using direct marketing through buying agents, buyer's representatives, responding to direct buyer enquiries generated via the various Promotion Councils or using other sources.

Indirect exports are not exports in reality. The exporter works as a vendor or supplier to an export house or a big trading company. For example, Tata International is a very big international trading company. Many local businessmen supply them goods that are then exported by Tata International under its own banner. The idea here is that since small businessmen cannot have access to international markets, and hence they seek the name of a bigger company to reach markets abroad. They are assured of regular orders provided they can supply quality goods at mutually agreed prices on scheduled delivery Periods.

1.4 EXPORT DOCUMENTATION IN INDIA

MEANING OF EXPORT DOCUMENTATION

The term export documentation refers to all documents prepared in connection with exports from the stage of receiving the order to the time when the goods are on the board of ship. These documents are issue by various organizations.

For examples: Customs regulations and exchange control forms are issued by the government or other authorized agencies, bills of lading and consignment dates are issued by carriers and insurance policy is obtained from insurance companies. The work relating to documentation has grown in size and volume in most of the countries in the world. The preparation of the documents needed for export business is a difficult task involving considerable amount of time, experience and skill. But in fact, the successful execution of an export transaction depends on the skill and expertise with which documents are handled. It is necessary that due care is exercised in the preparation and negotiation of export documents.

Export documentation in India has evolved a great deal particularly since 1990. Efforts are on a faster track to streamline and modernise the system further. Prior to 1990, the documentation was all manual and not at all coordinated. The result was lot of delays and mistakes, rendering the task very clumsy, repetitive and truly frustrating. India adopted the ADS in 1991. ADS refer to Aligned Documentation System, which is the internationally accepted documentation system.

The export documentation framework in India can be classified into following two categories.

  i.   Commercial documents

  ii.   Regulatory documents

COMMERCIAL DOCUMENTS

Commercial Documents is a "Custom of Trade" in International commerce. The exporters/importers use these documents to discharge their respective legal and other incidental responsibilities under sales contract. Commercial documents can be divided into:

  (a)   Principal commercial documents

  (b)   Auxiliary commercial documents

Principal commercial documents:

These are the main documents essential for an export and are required:

- To effect physical transfer of goods and title to the goods from exporter to buyer
- To realize export sales proceeds
- Commercial invoice (and the invoice prescribed by the importer)
- Packing list

- Certificate of Inspection
- Certificate of insurance/insurance policy
- Bill of Lading/Airway bill/Combined transport document
- Certificate of Origin
- Bill of exchange
- Shipment advice

Auxiliary commercial Documents:

These documents are required to prepare/procure the principal commercial documents .The different Auxiliary commercial Documents are:

- Proforma invoice
- Shipping instructions
- Insurance declaration
- Intimation for Inspection
- Shipping order
- Mate's receipt
- Application for certificate or origin
- Letter to bank for negotiation/collection of documents

REGULATORY DOCUMENTS

Regulatory documents are legal documents which prescribed by various government departments/bodies for compliance of formalities under relevant laws governing export transactions these include:

- Exchange Control Declaration Form-GR Form
- Freight Payment Certificate
- Insurance Premium Payment Certificate
- ARE I / ARE II Forms
- Shipping Bill/Bill of Export
- Port Trust Copy of Shipping Bill/Export Application/Dock Challan
- Receipt of payment of Port Charges
- Vehicle Ticket

A detailed description of all the commercial documents is given below:

1. **Commercial Invoice:** Commercial Invoice is the basic and most important document in an export transaction and the exporter has to take great to care prepare this document. A commercial invoice must provide complete and accurate information. A slight mistake on the part of the exporter would cause spending of more cost. The exporter has to submit the following details:

    - Invoice number with date,
    - details of the consigner and buyer (if the buyer is other than the consignee),
    - buyer's order number with date,
    - country of origin of the goods,
    - country of final destination,
    - terms of payment and delivery,
    - pre-carriage details(road/rail),
    - place of receipt by pre-carrier,
    - vessel/flight number,
    - port of loading,
    - port of discharge,
    - final destination,
    - marks and numbers,
    - container number,
    - number and kind of packaging,
    - detailed description of goods,
    - quantity,
    - Rate and total amount chargeable.
    - a commercial invoice contains the complete details of the export order right from order number to quantity,
    - rate,
    - Packaging, mode of dispatch and shipping particulars.
    - Normally,

- the trade practice is to raise and send a Proforma invoice to the buyer for his approval,

- Once the order has been finalized. On receipt of the approved Proforma invoice,

- The exporter can use it as part of the export contract.

- The commercial invoice then becomes easier to prepare on the basis of

The objectives of Commercial invoice are:

- It serves as the exporter's bill as it indicates the total chargeable amounts.

- It provides both the consignor's and consignee's details and the order number.

- It gives the complete details of goods being shipped, corresponding to the export order and letter of credit.

- As per the export order, the exporter is required to ship the exact quantity in the required packing. The invoice includes both the quantity and packing, which must be in strict be in accordance with the specifications of the export contract.

- It includes the terms of delivery and payment that are to be as per the letter or credit/export contract.

Segments of the commercial invoice:

1. **Exporter:** The detail of the exporter appears on the top left hand corner of the commercial invoice. The exporter is required to give his name and complete address specifying the city, state and county along with his phone and fax numbers. The purpose is to establish the identity of the shipper.

2. **Consignee:** This requires the details, of the name and complete address of the party to whom the goods are being consigned.

3. **Buyer:** Usually, the buyer and the consignee are the same; however, in cases where the buyer is different from the consignee, his details, that is, the buyer's name and complete address is to be provided.

4. **References and Numbers with date:** The relevant references such as exporter's quotation number with date,

invoice number with date, buyer's order number with date have to be accurately filled in.

5. **Country of Origin of Goods:** The exporter has to mention the name of the country where the goods have actually been produced.

6. **Country of Final Destination:** This provides the name of the country where the goods will be finally delivered.

7. **Terms of Delivery and payment:** Here the details of the terms of delivery like FOB, C&F, CIF etc. and the terms of payment such as L/C (letter of credit), D/A)(documents against acceptance), D/P (documents against Payment) etc.

8. **Pre-Carriage By:** The name of the carrier/mode of transport used to bring the goods from the place of origin to the place where these are accepted by the pre-carrier.

9. **Place of Receipt by Pre-Carrier:** The name of the place where goods are accepted by the Pre-carrier are mentioned in this segment.

10. **Vessel/Flight Number:** The name and number details of the shipping vessel or the aircraft carrier being used for the shipment is included.

11. **Port of Loading:** The name of the port where goods are loaded0on board ship or flight is required to be provided.

12. **Port of Discharge:** The name of the port where goods are finally offloaded (airport or Seaport) is to be filled in this section.

13. **Final Destination:** This segment contains the name of the place that is the final destination of the shipment. This will not mean the port of discharge but the final destination from the port of discharge in the buyer's country.

14. **Mark Numbers and Container Number:** This segment shows the various marks and numbers that are required to be put on the packed cargo. If containers are being used, then the container numbers are also required.

15. **Number and Kind of Packages:** Here, the type of packages being shipped such as cartons, bales, bags, drums,

crates etc, and the total number of such packages being shipped are to be provided.

16. **Description of Goods:** The detailed description of goods being shipped is to be put in this section. The description has to be the same as required in the export order/letter of credit. If more than one type of goods is being sent, the description of each is required to be given against the respective number and kind of packages.

17. **Quantity, Rate and Amount:** These columns must show the quantity and the respective rates of each item being exported and the total amount chargeable, both in figures and words. The quantities and rates have to be the same as seen in the export contract.

18. **Signature with Date:** The invoice must in the end, have the signatures with Date of the exporter or his authorized representatives. The invoice will be complete and effective, only if the signature with date is done

At times, the importing buyer may ask for specific commercial invoices as per the customs/requirements of their countries:

(i) **Consular Invoice:** Some countries use consular invoice as a non-tariff barrier. The exporter is required to get the commercial invoice verified by the Embassy/Consulate of the importer's country in his (exporter's) country. This certification is done by way of seal/stamp from the Commercial section of the Embassy/Consulate on payment of the requisite processing fee. For example, many of the Middle East Countries require this verification for their imports from India.

(ii) **Legalized Invoice:** The exporter is required to get the commercial invoice certified by the local chamber of commerce in the exporting country to verify the correctness of the invoice. Once attested, this commercial invoice becomes legalized for the importing country.

(iii) **Customs Invoice:** The importing country requires the commercial invoice to be prepared in its own prescribed format, usually for safeguard against dumping activity. The information required is almost the same and the exporter is required to self-attest such invoices.

2. Packing List:

The packing list includes the details of number of packages: quantity packed in each of them, the weight and measurement of each package and the net and gross weight of the total consignment. Net weight refers to the actual weight of the items and gross weight means the weight of the items plus the weight of the packing material. It contains almost all the information like the commercial invoice except the rate and total amount. It excludes the financial part of the transaction but concentrates on the physical and material part.

When the shipment consists of one item in a single pack, the packing information is incorporated in the invoice itself. However, as a general trade custom, both the documents are used irrespective of the size of the shipment.

The packaging list serves a useful purpose for the exporter while dispatching the consignment as a crosscheck of goods sent. For the port personnel, it comes handy while planning the loading and offloading of cargo. It is also an essential document for the customs authorities as they can carry out the physical examination of cargo and conduct checks on the weight and measurements of the goods smoothly against the declarations made by the exporter in the packing list.

Shipping Instructions

This document serves as a checklist of the exporter's instructions to the shipping company regarding a particular shipment.

Export Promotion Authority

3. Certificate of Inspection:

This is the certificate issued by the EIA after it has conducted the pres-shipment inspection of goods for export provided the goods fall under the notified category of goods requiring compulsory pre-shipment inspection.

4. Certification of Insurance/Insurance Policy:

Insurance is an important area in the export business as the stakes are usually very high. Protection needs to be taken in the form of insurance cover for the duration of transit of goods from the exporter to the importer.

Regular exporters normally opt for an open insurance policy and as they make a shipment, they are required to file an insurance declaration with the insurance company. An open policy is a kind of policy to insure a certain class or classes of goods to be shipped to specified destinations during a period of time, usually twelve months. Against this declaration, the insurance company issues an insurance certificate, which is a negotiable instrument. The Policy covers all the terms and conditions of the cargo insurance whereas a certificate issued under an open policy serves as an evidence of insurance of goods shipped.

5. Bill of Lading/Airway Bill/Combined Transport Document:

These documents are also known as Transport Documents.

Bill of Lading is issued when goods are shipped using ocean (marine) transport, i.e. ships. When the exporter finally hands over the goods to the shipping company for loading on board the ship for transport to their foreign destination, the shipping company issues a set of Bills of Lading to the exporter. This set serves multiple purposes. It is a receipt signifying physical acceptance of cargo by the shipping company and also a contract of carriage between the exporter and the shipping company for transport of the goods to their designated destination. In addition, the bill of lading also works as a document of title to the goods. The importer gets the right to take possession of the merchandise in his own country only if he possesses the bill of lading. This document is the instrument used for passing the ownership right or title of the goods to the buyer by the exporter.

A bill of lading is a negotiable instrument as it is transferable by endorsement and delivery. It also serves some non-negotiable purposes. Therefore, it is always issued as a set containing both negotiable and non-negotiable copies.

A bill of lading can be 'freight paid', where the freight is prepaid or 'freight to pay', where the freight depending upon or is to be collected at destination. Where the freight The shipping company will stamp the bill lading as freight prepaid in case the exporter has already paid the freight at the port of loading and the bill of lading will be marked as freight collected or freight to pay if the freight has not been paid and is required to be collected from the importer at the port of discharge.

Types of Bill of Lading:

- An On Board or Shipped Bill of lading signifies that the goods have been placed on board the ship. Such B/Ls are required in case of FOB (Free on Board) shipments.

- Received for Shipment Bill of Lading signifies that the shipping company has received the goods for shipment. Goods are waiting for shipment and are under the custody of the shipping line. Such B/Ls will work in case of FAS (Free alongside Ship) shipments.

- A Clean Bill of Lading does not contain any negative remark on either the quality of goods or on the physical conditions of the packaging of the merchandise received by the shipping company. Importers worldwide insist on such B/Ls.

- A Dirty or Claused Bill of Lading carries a remark put by the shipping company regarding the damage to the goods or their packaging.

- A Stale Bill of Lading is presented by the importer at the port of discharge late and as a result he may be required to pay fines and ward housing charges, etc. If this delay is caused due to exporter's late dispatch of documents, the importer is likely to penalize him.

- A Transshipment Bill of Lading is required when goods are required to the transshipped. However, the original carrier who issues such a bill takes on the role of an agent in all subsequent journeys and thus cannot be held responsible for any loss/damage to the cargo during such subsequent transport.

- A Through Bill of lading is required where goods are to move from one carriage to another. This B/L acts as a combined transport document where the original carrier takes on the role of the Principal carrier and thus becomes responsible for the total journey for loss/ damage to the cargo.

- The shipping company issues a Charter Party Bill of lading in cases of charter shipping. Such B/Ls require specific authorization in the L/C for purposes of negotiation.

- A Short Forms Bill of Lading contains all the elements of a B/L except contract of affreightment. Banks do not accept such bills for negotiation unless expressly prohibited by the L/C.

- A House Bill of lading, also called a freight forwarders' bill of lading, is issued by the freight forwarder, consolidator or a NVC (non-vessel carrier). It is a non-negotiable document containing the names, addresses of the parties and specific description of the goods shipped.

1. Airway Bill:

Airway bill is a bill of lading used when the goods are shipped using air transport. It is also known as an air consignment note or airway bill of lading. It is similarly to the ocean bill of lading on two counts. One, it too serves as a receipt of goods by the carrier and two, it also works as a contract of carriage between the shipper and the carrier. However, unlike it does not serve as a document of title to the goods. Hence, it is a non-negotiable document.

The goods will be delivered to the party named as consignee in the AWB without need of any further formalities, once the importer obtains customs clearance. Therefore, an exporter is advised to ensure the payment receipt, as it is quite risky to consign goods through air direct to the importer.

As per **IATA (International) Air Transport Association)** norms, an airway bill is issued as a set of 12 copies, having three originals as explained below:

1. First Original green in color. It is meant for the carrier issuing it and is to be signed by the exporter or his agent.

2. Second Original is pink colored and is meant for the importer (consignee) and therefore accompanies the shipment through to the final destination and is signed by the carrier or his agent.

3. Signed by the air carrier after goods have been accepted for airfreight and handed over to the consignor.

Airway bill is a very important document when goods are sent through air. It serves him all-important purpose of tracking the shipment and is also required at the time of customs clearance.

4. Combined Transport Document: Is also known as Multi-modal transport document. The concept of combined transport has gained importance before the popularization of containers.

5. Containerization has made it possible to move the goods from the place of origin, i.e., the factory or warehouse, to its final destination that is the buyer's premises in the foreign country. Containers, in fact are also used in domestic transportation in India. Indian Railways have their door-to-door delivery Service. The goods are transported in containers from one country to the other using different modes of transport. From the exporter's premises, the containers are loaded on trailers (road transport), which then use rail transport for carriage up to the port of loading and finally these are put on board the vessel. Likewise, in the foreign country too, the containers travel up to the importers premises using multiple or combined modes of transport.

The combined transport document covers the total journey of cargo using the various transport modes.

6. Certificate of origin: This document serves as a proof of the country of origin of goods for the importer in his country. Importing countries usually require the certificate of original to be produced at the time of customs clearance of import cargo. It also plays an important part in computing the liability and rate of import duty in the importing country. This certificate declares the details of goods to be shipped and the country where these goods are grown, manufactured or produced, such goods need to have substantial value-addition in the country of export so as to become eligible to certification of this nature. Certificate of origin has the preferential duty treatment attached to it provided it falls under the GSP Category. The Certificate of Origin can be either preferential or non-preferential.

   a) **Non-Preferential:** The local chamber of commerce in the country of export normally issues such a certificate of origin. It serves only as a proof of country of origin and does not offer any duty benefits to the importing countries. The exporter is required to make an application to the local chamber of commerce in a prescribed format and the chamber upon scrutiny of this application will issue the certificate of origin.

b) **Preferential:** These are required by importing countries offering concessional (preferential) import duties to import from certain countries under certain trade agreements. The following preferential certificates of origin currently applicable for exports from India are:

i) **Generalized System of Preferences (GSP):**

Under this system many developed countries like the US,Japan, Switzerland, Canada, Hungary, EU, Norway and New Zealand offer concessional tariffs to developing nations. This instrument is non-contractual in nature and the offer is made on a unilateral and non-reciprocal basis. GSP Schemes are reviewed and updated on a timely basis to give details of specific benefits available under particular product categories by the above countries. Usually, these benefits are made available to exporters on providing relevant information in a prescribed GSP form.

ii) **Global System of Trade preferences (GSTP):**

GSTP refers to an arrangement between developing nations under which concessional tariffs are provided on a reciprocal basis. India has such arrangements with many other developing countries. For availing these preferences, exporters in India can obtain certificate of origin under GSTP from EIA (Export Inspection Agency), which is the sole agency authorized to issue these certificates.

iii) Other preferential systems exist under the SAARC Preferential Trade Agreement (SAPTA), Bilateral Preferential Trading Agreement with Afghanistan, Indo-Sri Lankan Free Trade Agreement etc.

Shipping Order:

A Shipping order is a reservation slip issued by the shipping company against the exporters or his agent's request for booking of ship space for a shipment. When the transport of cargo, is by air this document is known as Carting Order.

Mate's Receipt:

The mate's receipt is a document given by the master of the ship to the port authorities for every shipment, as soon as the goods are received on board. The exporter must then collect this receipt either himself or through his authorized agent from the port authorities by paying all charges due to them. The shipping company issues the bill of lading to the exporter only against the mate's receipt. Is not a document of title? But is merely a receipt of goods. However, it is a very important document and without this, the exporter will not be able to obtain the title document to the goods, that is, the bill of lading. Therefore, the exporter is best advised to obtain the mate's receipt from the port authorities soon after the goods have been placed on board. Any delay may further result in greater delays leading to unwanted losses.

7. **Bill of Exchange:**   It is also known as a Draft, This is a common instrument for payment realization. It is a written unconditional order for payment from a drawer to a drawee, directing the drawee to pay a specified amount of money in a given currency to the drawer or a named payee at a fixed or determinable future date.

   The exporter is the drawer and he draws (prepares and signs) this unconditional order in writing upon the importer (drawee), asking him to pay a certain sum of money either to himself or to his nominee (endorsee). This order could be made for payment on demand is called a bill of exchange at sight or payment at a future date, called a usance bill of exchange. Usually, sight bills of exchange are used with Documents against Payments (D/P) method of receiving payment and usance bills of exchange are used for Documents against Acceptance (D/A) system. Since both these systems do not provide any security to the exporter regarding payment realization, these bills, in actual practice, are drawn under a letter of credit to ensure guarantee of payment. Usance bills of exchange are drawn for periods ranging from one to six months. These are negotiable and are usually discounted by the exporter.

8. The shipment advice is a document sent by the exporter to the importer, which contains the shipmen details and serves

as advance intimation of the shipment. This facilitates the important to make arrangements for the delivery.

Letter to Bank for Negotiation/Collection of Documents: This is a standard letter covering various instructions that an exporter must give to his bank at the time of submitting shipment documents concerning the negotiation/collection of documents.

The regulatory documents:

1. **Exchange Control Declaration Forms:**   As per the Foreign Exchange Management (Export of Goods and Services) Act, 2000, all exporters from India excepting those exporting to Nepal and Bhutan, are required to submit an exchange control declaration form in the prescribed format. The purpose behind this declaration is to ensure timely realization of export proceeds by the exporters and to track the defaulters.

2. **Freight Payment Certificate:**   This certificate is an evidence of freight payment. It certifies that due freight has been paid by the exporter. It is an equivalent of freight receipt.

3. **Insurance Premium Payment Certificate:**   This document certifies the payment of insurance Premium.

4. **ARE I / ARE II Forms:**   These are forms pertaining to Central Excise clearance. These are used only by those exporters who are governed by Central Excise.

5. **Shipping Bill/Bill of Export:**   This is the most important document required by customs authorities for permitting exports. It is called a shipping bill in case of export by sea/air and a bill of export when the export is done using land transport. The goods are allowed to enter the port only after the custom officials have stamped the shipping bill. It contains complete details of the shipment including name of exporter, name of importer, description of goods, port of loading, port of discharges marks, number, quantity, FOB value, country of destination, name of the vessel or flight number. Etc.

   Shipping bills can be of the following types:

   a) Shipping bill for dutiable goods

   b) Shipping bill for duty-fee goods

   c) Shipping bill for claiming duty drawback

- **Port Trust Copy of Shipping Bill/Export Application/ Dock Challan:** This form is the same as shipping bill. However, the purpose here is to assess the various port and dock charges. This is used in sea shipments.

- **Receipt of Payment of Prot Charges:** This is the receipt issued by the Port Trust Authority on payment of port dues by the exporter.

- **Vehicle Ticket:** It serves the purpose of an entry pass for the exporter to get his export cargo inside the port for export to its final destination.

- **Additional Documents/Certificates:** In addition to the various documents/certificates discussed above, there may be a need of some additional documents/certificates. These are briefly described below:

- **Blacklist Certificate:** This is required only in those specific cases where the importing country is at war or has hostile relations with another country and wants to make sure that the exporter is not in any way touching that country for purposes of fulfilling this order.

- **Antiquity Certificate:** This certificate is needed only in those cases where goods are being exported as antiques and the importer wants their authenticity checked. In India, Archaeological Survey of India is authorized to issue such certificates.

- **Health/Veterinary/Sanitary Certificate:** Many importing countries require such certificates particularly in case of imports of foodstuff, livestock, hides, marine products, etc. to safeguard against the dangers of diseases and health hazards. The exporter has to get the required certification from the respective health, veterinary or sanitary authorities, before he is able to dispatch his goods.

- **Fumigation Certificate:** Certain importing countries require fumigation of the cargo before it is allowed to enter their limits. This is again needed for cargo like plants and weeds, to ensure safety against spread of harmful virus. The exporter has to not only got the fumigation done but has to also submit a certificate from the prescribed agency to that effect.

DEPARTMENT OF COMMERCE

Functional Divisions in the Department of Commerce that play important role in exports:

Administrative and General Division

i)   Finance Division

ii)   Economic Division

iii) Trade Policy Division

iv)   Foreign Trade Territorial Division

v)   Export Products Divisions

vi)   Export Industries Division

vii) Export Services Division

Autonomous Bodies

1. **Commodity boards:**

    There are five Statutory Commodity Boards under the Department of Commerce. These Boards are responsible for production, development and export of tea, coffee, rubber, spices and tobacco respectively.

2. **Export Inspection Council, New Delhi:**

    The Export Inspection Council, a statutory body, is responsible for the enforcement of quality control and compulsory pre-shipment inspection of various exportable commodities covered under the Export (Quality Control and Inspection) Act, 1963.

3. **Indian Institute of Foreign Trade, New Delhi:**

    The Indian Institute of Foreign Trade, registered under the Societies Registration Act, is engaged in the following activities.

    i)   Training of personnel in modern techniques of international trade.

    ii)   Organization of research in problems of foreign trade.

    iii) Organization of marketing research, area survey, commodity surveys and market surveys.

    iv)   Dissemination of information arising from its activities relating to research and market studies.

4. **Indian Institute of Packaging, Mumbai:**

    The Indian Institute of Packaging is registered under the Societies Registration Act. The main aims of the Institute are to undertake research of raw materials for the packaging industry, to organize training programmers on packaging technology, to stimulate consciousness of the need for good packaging etc.

5. **Indian Diamond Institute:**

The Indian diamond Institute (IDI) is registered under the Societies Registration Act. It was established in 1978 with the objective of strengthening and improving the availability of trained manpower for the gems and jewellery industry by conducting various diploma/post diploma level courses in this field. Some of the important courses conducted by IDI for the gems and jewellery sector include:

i)   Diploma in diamond processing

ii)   Diploma in diamond trade management

iii)   Diploma in gemology

iv)   PG Diploma in diamond technology

v)   PG Diploma in gemology

vi)   PG Diploma in jewellery designing, manufacturing and appraising The Institute is financed by the Government of India. Ministry of Commerce and the Gem and Jewellery Export Promotion Council. The Institute has been striving to augment its resources by undertaking consultancy and job works.

6. **Export Promotion Councils:**

There are at present eleven Export Promotions Councils under the administrative control of the Ministry of Commerce. These Councils are registered as non-profit organizations under the Companies Act/Societies Registration Act. The Export Promotion Councils perform both advisory and executive functions. These Councils are also the registering authorities under the Export and Import Policy 1997-2002.Theses Councils have been assigned the role and functions under the said Policy.

7. **Federation of Indian Export Organizations, New Delhi:**

The Federation of Indian Export Organizations (FIEO), New Delhi, is an apex body of various export Promotion organizations and institutions. It also functions as a primary servicing agency to provide integrated assistance to the government recognized export houses/trading houses and as a central coordinating agency in respect of export promotional efforts in the field of consultancy services in the country. FIEO organizes seminars and arranges participation in various exhibitions in India and abroad. FIEO is also involved in dissemination of awareness on modern information technology through the internet and home page of EDI and Electronic commerce among the exporters.

8. **Indian Council of Arbitration, New Delhi:**

The Indian Council of Arbitration, set up under the Societies Registration Act, Promotes arbitration as a means of settling commercial disputes and popularizes the concept of arbitration among the traders, particularly those engaged in international trade. The Council, a non-profit service organization, is a grantee institution of the Ministry. The main objectives of the council are to promote the knowledge and use of arbitration and provide arbitration facilities for amicable and quick settlement of commercial dispute with a view to maintaining the smooth flow of trade, particularly, our export trade on a sustained and enduring basis.

9. **Marine Products Export Development Authority, Cochin:**

The Marine Products Export Development Authority, a statutory body, is responsible for the development of the marine products industry with special reference to exports.

10. **Agricultural and Processed Food products Export Development Authority, New Delhi:**

The Agricultural and Processed Food products Export Development Authority is also a statutory body which serves as the focal point for agricultural exports, particularly the marketing of processed foods in value added form.

11. **Public Sector Undertakings:**

The following trading/service corporations function under the administrative control of the Ministry of Commerce.

i)   State Trading Corporation of India Ltd., (Cashew Corporation on India Ltd., being merged as a division in STC).

ii) Mineral and Metal Trading Corporation of India Ltd. And its subsidiary Mica Trading Corporation of India Ltd.

iii) Projects and Equipment Corporation of India Ltd.

iv) Spices Trading Corporation of India Ltd.,

v)   Export Credit Guarantee Corporation of India Ltd.

vi)   Indian Trade Promotion Organization (ITPO).

Advisory Bodies

1.   **Board of Trade:**

There is a Board of Trade under the Ministry of Commerce which was constituted on May 5, 1989, to provide a forum for ensuring a continuous dialogue with trade and industry in respect of major developments in the field of international trade. The Chairman of the Board of Trade is the Commerce Minister and Director General of Foreign Trade is the Member Secretary. The membership of the Board includes the Governor, the Reserve Bank of India, Secretaries of the Ministries of Commerce, Industry, Finance and Textiles, Special Secretary, Prime Minister's Office; President of FICCI, ASSOCHAM, CII, FIEO, FASSI; representative of trade and industry and a few specialists.

2.   **Export Promotion Board:**

There is an Export Promotion Board under the Chairmanship of the Cabinet Secretary to provide policy and infrastructural support through greater coordination among the concerned Ministries for boosting the growth of exports.

The representation received from various Chambers of Commerce, organizations and experts and examined by the various divisions of the Ministry and the emerging issues are taken up with the concerned Ministries. In case of disagreement, the matter is placed before the Export Promotion Board for a final decision. The Export Promotion Board takes important decisions regarding electronics, textiles and garments, plastic and gems and jewellery, telecommunications, infrastructure, toys and engineering exports sectors, etc.

1.5   EXPORT FINANCE IN INDIA IS AVAILABLE IN TWO CATEGORIES:

- Pre-shipment finance
- Post –Shipment Finance

Pre-shipment finance deals with the finance schemes available before the shipment has been made. Post-Shipment finance, deals with credit available after the goods have been shipped. Both stages are crucial for the exporter. He needs finance to get the procurement/product ion going after receipt of the export order. Money is also needed to fund the working capital expenses for day-to-day activities. Post-shipment finance is required to take care of the financial needs after the shipment is over.

Pre-shipment finance facilities offer liquidity to the exporter to procure raw materials, carry out processing, packing. Transporting and ward housing of the goods to be exported, Post-shipment finance provides credit facility from the date of shipment of the goods to the time export payment is realized.

Need for Export Finance:

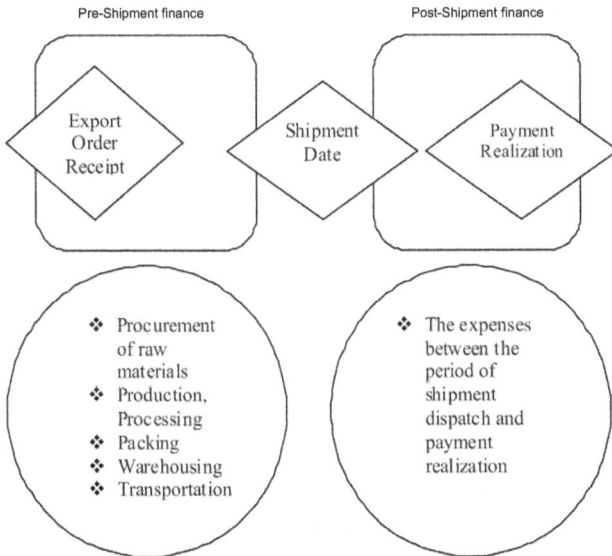

International trade is fiercely competitive. The exporter needs to have a competitive edge over other supplies from various countries. To this end, access to export finance at competitive rates of interest will immensely serve the exporter's cause. Both types of finance facilities are important. Pre-shipment finance, as we have already seen, helps the exporter to get started with procurement and production. Timely availability of funds will define the exporter's ability to ship the right quality of goods at the right time. Post-shipment finance assumes importance in view of the exporter's need to extend credit to the importers to remain competitive. This period, when goods have gone and payment is yet to come, poses several liquidity challenges to the exporter. Post-shipment finance provides effective solutions to the liquidity woes of the exporter.

Role of RBI in Export Finance:

The Reserve Bank of India, the Central Bank of our country does not directly provide finance to the exporters. RBI has developed various schemes to encourage commercial banks to provide export credit to the export sector. The schemes of RBI are: (a) Export Bills Credit Scheme; 1963; (b) Pre-shipment Credit Scheme 1969; (c) Export Credit Interest Subsidy Scheme 1968; (d) Refinance under DBK Credit Scheme 1976.

(a) *Export Bill Credit Scheme:*
Under this scheme, RBI used to grant advances to scheduled banks against export bills, maturing within 180 days. Now, this scheme is not in operation.

(b) *Pre-shipment Credit Scheme:*
Under this scheme, RBI provides refinance facilities to scheduled banks that provide pre-shipment loans to bonafide exporters.

(c) *Export Credit Interest Subsidy Scheme :*
Under this scheme, RBI provides interest subsidy of minimum 1.5 per cent to banks that provide export finance to exporters, provided, the banks charge interest to exporters within the ceiling prescribed by RBI. The subsidy is given both against packing and post-shipment.

(d) *Duty Drawback Credit Scheme:*
Under this, the exporters can avail interest free advances from the Bank up to 90 days against shipping bills provisionally certified by customs authorities towards a refund of customs duty. These advances of commercial banks are eligible for refinance from RBI.

Apart from the above mentioned scheme, the Reserve Bank of India also approves or sanctions applications made by the exporters for:

(a) Allotment of Exporters 'Code Number, which is a must for every exporter,

(b) Extension of time limit for realization of export proceeds.

(c) Reduction in invoice price of export goods. (d) Fixation of commission to overseas consignee or agents.

(e) Provision of blanket permit where a lump sum exchange is released for a number of purposes.

(f)   Remittances abroad in respect of advertising, legal expenses, etc.

(g)   Appointments of foreign nationals as technical and non-technical personnel in Indian firms.

(h)   Appointment of non-residents as directors of Indian companies.

(i)   Any other matter relating to foreign trade that requires clearance from Exchange Control department of RBI.

(j)   Clearance in respect of joint-venture abroad.

Role of EXIM Bank in Export Finance:

The Export-Import Bank of India came into existence on January, 1, 1982 and started functioning from March 1, 1982. It has its headquarters in Mumbai and its branches of offices in important cities in India and abroad.

EXIM Bank was established for the purpose of financing medium and long term loans to the exporters thereby promoting foreign trade in the country. It took over the functions of international wing of IDBI. The main objectives of EXIM Bank are as follows:

(a)   Providing financial assistance (medium and long term) to exporters and importers.

(b)   Functioning as the principal financial institution for co-ordinating the working of institutions engaged in providing export finance

(c)   Promotion of foreign trade of India.

(d)   To deal with all matters that may be considered to be incidental or conducive to the attainment of above objectives.

The services rendered by EXIM Bank to the exporters can be discussed under two heads, viz.

• Fund Based Service, and

• Non-Fund Based Service.

Fund Based Service:

Under this, the EXIM Bank renders assistance to

(i)   Indian Exporters

(ii)   Overseas Buyers and Agencies; and

(iii)   Indian Commercial Banks.

Assistance to Indian Exporters:

(a)   Provides direct financial assistance to exporters on deferred payment terms.

(b)   Finance export and import of machinery and equipment on lease basis.

(c)   Finances Indian joint ventures in foreign countries.

(d)   Provides pre-shipment finance to eligible exporters for procuring raw materials and other inputs required to produce machinery and equipment to be exported.

(e)   Offers credit facilities to —Deemed Exports.

(f)   Provides Computer Software Exporters foreign exchange loan subject to RBI clearance.

(g)   Provides finance facility against deferred credit to exporters of consultancy, technology and other services.

(h)   Provides finance to Indian exporters to undertake various export marketing activities in India and abroad through Export Marketing Fund (EMF).

(i)   Operates Export Development Fund (EDF) to finance techno-economic survey / research or any other study for the development of Indian Exports.

Assistance to Overseas Buyers and Agencies:

(a)   EXIM Bank offers_Overseas Buyer's Credit facility 'to foreign importers for import of Indian capital goods and related services with repayment spread over a period of years.

(b)   Long term finance is also provided under Lines of Credit to finance government and financial institution abroad, which in turn, extend finance to importers of their country to buy Indian capital goods.

(c)   It provides relending facility to overseas banks to make available term finance to their clients for import of Indian goods.

Assistance to Indian Commercial Banks:

(a)   EXIM Bank provides refinance facilities so as to enable commercial banks to offer credit to Indian exporters who extend term credit to importers.

(b)   It offers Export Bills Rediscounting facility to commercial banks in India so that it helps commercial banks to fund post-shipment credit extended to Indian exporters.

Non-Fund Based Services

Assistance is divided into two groups:

(i)   Financial Guarantees and Bonds,

(ii)   Advisory and other services.

Financial Guarantees and Bonds:

EXIM Bank provides non-fund based assistance in the form of guarantees in the nature of bit brands, performance guarantees etc.

Advisory and other Services:

(a)   It advises Indian companies in executing contracts abroad, and on sources of overseas financing.

(b)   It advises Indian exporters on global exchange control practices.

(c)   The EXIM Bank offers financial and advisory services to Indian construction project abroad.

(d)   It advises small-scale manufacturer on export markets and products.

(e)   It provides access to Euro financing sources and global credit sources to Indian exporters.

(f)   It assists the exporters under forfeiting scheme.

1.6   COMMERCIAL BANKS

Commercial banks in order to improve the exports, offer export finance at special rates to the exporters in tune with the export promotion initiatives of the government to boost exports. Concessional interest rates and liberal schemes have been introduced in India by the Commerce Ministry through the Reserve Bank of India (RBI)

The risks are large today due to political and economic changes that are sweeping the world. An outbreak of war or civil war may block or delay payment for the goods supplied. Tariff & non tariff restrictions are imposed. Economic difficulties or balance of payment problems may lead a country to impose restrictions on either import of certain goods, or on transfer of payments for goods imported. In additions, one has to contend with the usual commercial risks of the foreign buyer going bankrupt, or losing his capacity to pay. Conducting export business in such conditions of uncertainty is carried on with danger.

The loss of a large payment be a great disaster for any exporter, whatever his prudence and competence. Too cautious of an attitude in anticipating & evaluating risks and selecting buyers may result in loss of hard-to –get business opportunities. Export credit insurance protects exporters from the consequences of payment default on account of adverse political and commercial developments, and to enable them to expand their business without any fear of loss.

Export credit insurance also seeks to create a favorable climate in which exporters can hope to get timely and liberal credit facilities from banks at home. For this purpose, export credit insurance provides guarantees to banks to protect them from the risk of loss inherent in granting various types of finance facilities of exporters. One such Corporation which provides guarantee is ECGC.

1.7   EXPORT CREDIT AND GUARANTEE CORPORATION (ECGC)

The Government of India set up the Export Risks Insurance Corporation (ERIC) in July, 1957 which was transformed into the Export Credit and Guarantee Corporation (ECGC) in 1964. The Corporation's name was once again changed to the present Export Credit Guarantee Corporation of India in 1983. ECGC is a company wholly owned by the Government of India. ECGC was mainly setup to provide export credit insurance. It functions under the administrative control of the Ministry of Commerce, and is managed by a Board of Directors representing Government, Banking, Insurance, Trade and Industry, etc.

The cover provided by ECGC is of four types:

i)   Standard policy issued to exporters to protect them against payment risks involved in exports on short term credit and Small Exporter's policy issued for the same purpose to exporters with small exports;

ii)   Specific policies designed to protect Indian firms against payment risks involved in (a) exports on deferred terms of payment (b) services rendered to foreign parties and (c) construction works and turnkey projects undertaken abroad.

iii)   Financial guarantees issued to banks in India to protect them from risks of loss involved in their extending financial support to exporters at the pre-shipment as well as post-shipment stages: and

iv)   Special schemes, viz, Transfer Guarantee meant to protect banks which add confirmation to a Letter of Credit opened by foreign banks, insurance cover for Buyer's Credit, Line of Credit, Overseas investment Insurance and Exchange Fluctuation Risk insurance.

Standard Policy:

Shipments (comprehensive risks) Policy, commonly known as the Standard Policy, is ideally suited to cover risks in respect of goods exported on short-term credit, i.e. credit not exceeding 180 days. This Policy covers both commercial and political risks from the date of shipment. It is issued to exporters whose anticipated export turnover for the next 12 months is more than Rs.25 lakhs. The appropriate policy for exporters with an anticipated turnover of less than Rs.25lakhs is the Small exporter's Policy.

Risks Covered Under the Policy

Under the Shipments (Comprehensive Risks) Policy, the Corporation covers from the date of shipment for the following risks;

Commercial risks

•   Insolvency of the buyer

•   Failure of the buyer to make the payment due within a specified period. Normally 4 months from the due date.

•   Buyer's failure to accept the goods, subject to certain conditions.

Political risks

•   Impositions of restrictions by the Government of the buyer's country, or any Government action which may block or delay the transfer of payment made by the buyer.

- War, Civil War, revolution or civil disturbances in the buyer's country, mew import restriction or cancellation of a valid import license.

- Interruption or diversion of voyage outside India resulting in payment of additional freight or insurance charges which cannot be recovered from the buyer.

Any other cause of loss occurring outside India, not normally insured in general by insurers, and beyond the control of both the exporter and the buyer.

Risks Not Covered

The policy does not cover losses due to the following risks:

- Commercial disputes including quality disputes raised by the buyers, unless the exporter obtains a decree from a competent court of law in the buyer's country in his favour;

- Causes inherent in the nature of the goods:

- Buyer's failure to obtain necessary import or exchange authorization from authorities in his country;

- Insolvency or default of any agent of the exporter or of the collecting bank;

- Loss or damage to goods which can be covered by general insurers;

- Exchange rate fluctuation;

- Failure of the exporter to fulfill the terms of the export contract or negligence on his part.

Risks Covered:

The risks covered may be broadly grouped into

(a)   Commercial risks, and

(b)   Political risks.

Commercial risks covered:

(i)   Insolvency of the buyer;

(ii)   buyer's protracted default to pay for goods accepted by him; and

(iii)   buyer's failure to accept goods subject to certain conditions.

Political risks covered:

(i)   Imposition of restrictions on remittances by the government in the buyer's country or any government action which may block or delay payment of the exporter;

(ii)   War, revolution or civil disturbances in the buyer's country;

(iii)   New import licensing restrictions or cancellation of a valid import license in the buyer's country;

(iv)   Cancellation of export license or imposition of new export licensing restrictions in India;

(v)   Payment of additional handling, transport or insurance charges occasioned by interruption or diversion of voyage which cannot be recovered from the buyer; and

(vi)   Any other cause of loss occurring outside India, not normally insured by commercial insurers, and beyond the control of the exporter and/ or the buyer.

Types of Policies

The policy issued may cover risks from the date of shipment or from the date of contract. In either case, the policy may cover both political and commercial risks (Comprehensive policy) or it may cover only political risks. Thus, the policy may be any one of the following:

(i)   Shipment (Comprehensive Risks) Policy;

(ii)   Shipment (Political Risks) Policy;

(iii)   Contract (Comprehensive Risks) Policy; or

(iv)   Contract (Political Risks) Policy,

Extent of Cover

ECGC normally pays 90 per cent of the losses on account of political or commercial risks. In the event of loss due to repudiation of contractual obligations by the buyer, ECGC indemnifies the exporter up to 90 per cent of the loss if final and enforceable decree against the overseas buyer is obtained in a competent court of law in the buyer's country. The corporation, at its discretion, may waive such legal action where it is satisfied that such legal action is not worthwhile and in that event losses are indemnified up to 60 per cent. Recoveries made after the payment of the claim are shared with the ECGC in the same proportion in which the loss was borne.

Small Exporter's Policy

The small exporter's policy is basically the standard policy, incorporating certain improvements in terms of cover. It is issued to exporters whose anticipated export turnover for the next 12 months does not exceed Rs.25 lakhs.

The small exporter's policy differs from the standard policy in the following respects:

(i)   Period of policy:

Issued for 12 months as against 24 months in the case of standard policy.

(ii)   Minimum premium:

The minimum premium payable is 0.3% of the anticipated turnover on DP and DA terms of payment, plus where the exporter seeks cover also for LC shipments, 0.10% of the anticipated turnover on LC terns or Rs.1, 000, whichever is higher.

(iii) Declaration of shipments:

Shipments need to be declared only twice in the seventh month and the thirteenth month.

(iv) Declaration of overdue payments:

Monthly declarations of all payments remaining overdue by more than 60 days from the due date, as against 30 days in the case of standard policy.

(v)   Percentage of cover:

95% for loss due to commercial risk and 100% if due to political risk. Cover is 90% in both cases in standard policy.

(vi) Waiting period of claim:

Two months as against four months in standard policy.

SPECIFIC POLICIES

Specific Shipment Policy (Short-term):

Specific Shipment Policy (Short-term) offers to cover one or more shipments only under a particular contract. Option is available to cover both commercial and political risks and only political risks. The risks covered are the same as under the standard Policy. A separate policy is available to cover shipments made under letter of credit against the risks of insolvency and default of the L/C opening bank and political risks. The percentage of cover is 80. The policy cover can be availed of by exporters who do not hold the Standard Policy or even by those holding it to cover the shipments specifically permitted to be excluded from the purview of the Standard Policy.

Specific Policy for Supply Contracts:

Specific policy for supply contracts covers exports of commodities for period beyond 180 days. The policy may take any of the following four forms:

(i)   Specific shipments (Comprehensive risks) Policy-to cover both commercial and political risks at the post-shipment stage;

(ii) Specific shipments (Political Risks) Policy-to cover only political risks at the post-shipment stage in cases where the buyer is an overseas Government or payments are guaranteed by a Government or by banks, or are made to associates;

(iii) Specific Contracts (Comprehensive Risks) Policy; and

(iv) Specific Contracts (Political Risks) Policy.

Contracts policy provides cover from the date of contract. Losses that may be sustained by an exporter at the pre-shipment stage due to frustration of contract are covered under this policy in addition to the cover provided by the Shipments policy.

Insurance Cover for Buyer's Credit & Lines of Credit:

Financial institutions in India, like those in several other countries, lend directly to buyers or financial institutions in developing countries for importing machinery and equipment from India. This kind of financing facilitates immediate payment to exporters and frees them from the problems of credit management as well as from the fear of loss on account of overseas credit risks.

Financing may take the form of Buyer's Credit or Line of Credit. Buyer's Credit is a loan extended by a financial institution, or a consortium of financial institutions, to the buyer for financing a particular export contract. Under Lines of credit, a loan is extended to government or financial institutions in the importing country for financing import of specified items from the lending country. ECGC has evolved schemes to protect financial institutions in India which extend these types of credit for financing exports from India. Insurance Agreement will be drawn up on a case-to-case basis, having regard to the terms of the credit.

Service policy

When Indian firms render services to foreign parties, they would be exposed to payment risks similar to those involved in export of goods. Services Policy offers protection to Indian firms against such payment risks. The policy has been designed broadly on the lines of ECGC insurance policies covering export of goods and is issued to cover specific transactions. Two types of policies are issued;

(a)   Specific Services contract (comprehensive Risks) Policy to cover commercial as well as political risks,

(b)   Specific Services Contract (Political Risks) Policy to cover political risks only. Where the contracts are with overseas governments or payments are guaranteed by overseas governments or are covered by bank guarantees/letters of credit, or are too associated, political risks policies issued. A wide range of services like technical or professional services, hiring or issuing can be covered under the policies.

Construction Works Policy:

ECGC's construction Works Policy covers civil construction jobs as well as turnkey projects involving supplies and services. It provides cover for all payments that fall due to the contractor under the contract. Two types of policies are available to cover contracts with

(i)   Government buyers, and

(ii)   Private buyers.

The former covers political risks in respect of contracts with overseas Governments or where the payments are guaranteed by Government. The latter covers comprehensive risks. In case of contracts with private employers, the policy may be issued to cover only political risks if the payments are guaranteed by a bank or covered by Letter of Credit.

Overseas Investment Insurance:

ECGC has evolved a scheme to provide protection for involvement of exporters in capital participation in overseas projects. Any investments made by way of equity capital or untied loan for the purpose of setting up or expansion of overseas projects will be eligible for cover under investment insurance. The investment may be either in cash or in the form of export of Indian capital goods and services. The cover would be available for the original investment together with annual dividends and interest payable.

Exchange Fluctuation Risk Cover Schemes:

The Exchange Fluctuation Risk Cover Schemes are intended to provide a measure of protection to exporters of capital goods, civil engineering contractors and consultants who have often to receive payments over a period of years for their exports construction work or services. Where such payments are to be received in foreign currency, they are open to exchange fluctuation risk and the forward exchange market does not provide cover for such deferred payments. The Exchange fluctuation Risk Cover is available for payments scheduled over a period of 12 months or more, up to a maximum of 15 years. Cover can be obtained from the date of bidding right up to the final installment.

Maturity Factoring Facility:

A new service provided by ECGC is Maturity Factoring Facility to the exporters. Under maturity factoring the factor initially undertakes only sales ledger administration and collection functions. The factor pays the amount of each invoice to the client at the end of the credit term or on the agreed maturity date. Under this facility ECGC renders the services of credit protection, sales ledger maintenance and collection. Export transaction involving credits to the buyer for a period not exceeding 180 days are eligible. The exporter's bank will discount the export bill in the usual way. The exporter has to remit factoring charges to ECGC through the bank. Bank can claim payment from ECGC, 15 days after the date if payment is not received from overseas buyer by them, ECGC will make payment about 10 days after that.

Benefits to banks:

1. The maturity factoring facility offered by ECGC does not disturb the existing system of banking arrangement.

2. Banks would be able to finance against the factored bills at zero risk, as they would be protected even in case where the non-payment is due to dispute between the exporter and the buyer.

3. As the discounting of the bill under the scheme is to be done by the exporters' bank, they would not face any hassle in adjusting advances granted at the packing credit stage.

SHIPMENTS COVERED:

The Shipments (Comprehensive Risks) Policy is meant to cover all the shipments that may be made by an exporter on credit terms during a period of 24 months ahead. In other words, an exporter is required to get the insurance provided by the Policy for each and every shipment that may be made by him in the next 24months on DP, DA or Open Delivery terms to all buyers other than his own associate. The policy cannot be issued for selected shipments, selected buyers or selected markets.

Exclusion of shipment covered:

An exporter may, exclude shipments made against advance payment, or those which are supported by irrevocable Letters of Credit, which carry the confirmation of banks in India, since he faces no risk in respect of such transactions. Where an exporter is dealing with several distinct items, ECGC may agree to exclude all shipments of certain agreed items, provided that what is offered for insurance consists of all items of allied nature and offers the Corporation a reasonable portion of the exporter's total business with a fair spread of risks.

SHIPMENTS AGAINST LETTERS OF CREDIT:

Confirmed by banks in India, payments under irrevocable Letters of Credit are subject to political risks. Exporter, therefore, will be well advised to get them also covered under the Policy. Such shipments, which are excluded from the scope of the Policy, can be covered under it if an exporter desires. Lower premium rates are applied to them because they do not involve commercial risk and only the Political risks have to be covered.

For shipments made against irrevocable letters of Credit, and exporter has option to obtain either political risks cover only or cover for comprehensive risks, i.e., for all political risks and the risk of insolvency or default of the bank opening the irrevocable Letter of Credit. In either case, cover will be provided by the Corporation only if the exporter agrees to get all the shipments made against irrevocable Letters of Credit covered under the Policy. Cover will not be available for selected transactions.

SHIPMENT TO ASSOCIATES:

Shipments to associates i.e. foreign buyers in whose business the exporter has a financial interest, are normally excluded from the policy. They can however, be covered against political risks under the Policy if an exporter so desires. Where the associate is a public limited company in which the exporter's share holding does not exceed 40%, cover can be provided against insolvency risks in addition to all the political risks.

SHIPMENTS MADE BY AIR:

When shipments are made by air, the buyers can to obtain delivery of the goods from the airlines before making payment of the bills or accepting them for payment. If the buyer fails to make the payment subsequently as per the contract, the risk of loss will not be covered under the Policy if premium has been paid on the shipment for Document against Payment or Document against Acceptance terms of payment. An exporter can however, get cover for such contingencies also if he obtains Credit Limit on such buyers on Open Delivery terms, and also pays premium at rates applicable to Open Delivery terms.

SHIPMENT MADE ON CREDIT EXCEEDING 180 DAYS:

The policy is meant to provide cover for shipments involving a credit period not exceeding 180 days. In exceptional cases however, cover may be granted for shipments with longer credit period, provided that such longer credits are justifiable for the export items concerned.

SHIPMENTS TO ASSOCIATES:

Shipments which are made to an overseas agent under an agreement that he will receive the goods as agent of the exporter and remit the proceeds on their being sold by him are excluded from the scope of the Policy.

However, if an exporter wants it, the Corporation can get them included under the Policy. Cover will be provided only against political risks, since the agent acts for the exporter. If, however, goods are sold ultimate buyers on credit terms, comprehensive risks cover can be provided for sales to such ultimate buyers if the exporter wants such cover.

RISKS COVERED UNDER ECGC:

Maximum Liability

The Policy is intended to cover all the shipments that may be made by an exporter in a period of 24 months ahead, the Corporation will fix its maximum liability under each Policy. The maximum liability is the limit up to which ECGC would accept liability for shipments made in each of the policy years, for both commercial and political risks. It will be advisable for exporters to estimate the maximum outstanding payments due from overseas buyers at any one time during the policy period, and to obtain the policy with maximum liability for such a value. The maximum liability fixed under the Policy can be enhanced subsequently, if required.

Credit Limits on Buyers

Commercial risks covered are subjected to a Credit Limit approved by the Corporation on each buyer to whom shipments are made on credit terms. The exporter has therefore, to apply for a suitable Credit Limit on each buyer on the basis of its own judgment of the credit worthiness of the buyer, ascertained from credit reports obtained from banks and specialized agencies abroad, the Corporation will approve a Credit Limit which is the limit up to which it will pay claim on account of losses arising from commercial risks. The Credit Limit is a revolving limit and once approved it will hold good for all shipments to the buyers as long as there is no gap of more than 12 months between two shipments. Credit limit is a limit on the value of shipment that may be made to him. Premium has therefore, to be paid on the full value of each shipment even where the value of the shipment of the total value of the bills outstanding for payment is in excess of the Credit Limit.

It will be advisable for exporters to see that the total value of the bills outstanding with the buyer at any one time is not out proportion to the Credit Limit. In cases where the Credit Limit that the Corporation is prepared to grant is far lower than the value of outstanding, exporters should discuss the problem with the Corporation.

Credit limits need not, be obtained if a shipment is made on DP or CAD terms, and if the value of the shipment does not exceed Rs, 5 Lakhs. Political as well as commercial risks will stand automatically covered for such shipments, the only qualification being that the claims will be paid on more than two buyers during the Policy period under this provision.

Restricted Cover Countries

For a large Majority of countries, the Corporation Places no limit for covering political risks. However, in the case of certain countries where the political risks are very high, cover for political as well as commercial risk is granted on a restricted basis. Policy holders intending to export to such countries are required to obtain specific approval of the Corporation for each shipment or contract in advance, preferably before concluding the contract.

Where Specific Approval is granted, it may be subjected to certain special conditions and in some cases, subjected to payment of a Specific Approval Fee Specific Approval Fee is payable in addition to the premium on the shipments. A portion of the Specific Approval Fee is refundable in the event of shipments not taking place, or if the payments are received before the expiry of the waiting period for claims,

Time for Payment of Claim

A claim will arise when any of the risks insured under the Policy materializes. If any overseas buyer becomes insolvent, the exporter becomes eligible for a claim one month after his loss is admitted to rank against the insolvent's estate, or after four months from the due date, whichever is earlier. In case of protracted default, the claim is payable after four months from the due date. Claims in respect of additional handling, transport or insurance charges incurred by the exporter because of interruption or diversion of voyage outside India are payable after proof of loss is furnished. In all other cases, claim is payable after four months from the date of the event causing loss.

Payment terms in International Trade Financing:

The international market is generally very competitive and sensitive and the credit facilities made available to the buyers are one of the important determinants of export business.

The extent to which credit must be extended to the importer depends on the sale terms. If the exporter gets cash in advance, there will not be any problem in respect of finance,; but this is not common, Even if the exporter gets the payment at the time of the shipment of the goods, he has to make his own arrangements to meet his financial needs at the pre-shipment stage. If the sale is on credit, as it usually is the exporter will be still more constrained financially.

It is therefore, necessary to make institutional credit available to the export sector to meet its pre-shipment and post-shipment financial requirements, for such credit facilities will enable requirements at the pre-shipment stage but also to extend reasonable credit facilities to foreign buyers.

Payment Terms:

Some knowledge of the important payment terms and methods of effecting payment would be useful to understand the export financing methods and process. As the payment terms are determined on the basis of the specific circumstances of the particular buyers and seller, it would be difficult to make way generalization about payment terms.

Cash in Advance:

The most advantageous payment term from the seller's point of view is the remittance with the order, or sometimes, before the shipment of goods. The remittance may be by draft, cheque, mail or telegraphic transfer. Very seldom is an importer prepared to make cash payments in advance; but in certain cases it becomes necessary. If the seller enjoys a monopoly position or if there is a seller's market, it is easy to obtain advance payment, but when the market is very competitive, it is very difficult to do so.

Open Account:

Under trading on open account, the exporter ships the goods with no financial documents to his advantages except the commercial invoice. Under this method, therefore, the seller carries the entire financial burden with little or no documentary evidence. Because of the great risks associated with the open account method, it is generally restricted. Indian exporters are allowed to abroad on the open account bases only with the special permission of the RBI. Normally this permission is given only to foreign companies operating in India.

Consignment Sale:

Under the consignment sale, the exporter consigns the goods to his agent representative in the foreign markets, who arranges for the sale of the goods and makes payments to the exporter, under this method, the exporter retains the title of the goods until the sale of the goods is affected in the foreign market. The consignment sale involves a number of risks as exchange rate fluctuations and the loss that may arise if the consignee is inefficient or is not sincere and honest.

Documents against payment:

In Documents against Payment also known as cash against documents, the exporter ships goods to the foreign buyer, but the documents giving title to the goods will be handed over to the buyers through the bank only on payment. Under this type of transaction, until and unless the buyer makes the payment, the ownership of the goods remains with the seller. The exporter may obtain bank finance against document against payment bills. If the bank is satisfied, it may finance the exporter payment bills, usually on a with recourse basis, so in the event of non-payment by the draw, the bank has recourse to the drawer.

Document on acceptance:

Under the documents against payment method, the documents and the title to the goods are handed over the buyer when he accepts the bill of exchange by signing it. The usance of the bills of exchange may be 30 days, 60 days or 90 days. The exporter, thus, extends credit to the importer for such periods, under the document on acceptance terms, the exporter relies on the honesty and credit worthiness of the buyer, and therefore this facility is normally extended only to parties who have proven business integrity and financial standing. Banks may finance to exporters by purchasing the document against payment bills with recourse.

Documentary letter of credit:

The documentary letter of credit covers the major part of the export business. A letter of credit is a document containing the guarantee of a bank to honor it by an exporter, under certain conditions and then to certain amounts.

Some of the important payment terms have been outlined above. The actual payment term adopted in a particular transaction is influenced by a number of factors, such as the individual circumstances of the buyer and the seller, the nature of the product, the profit margin customs of the trade, the organization of the firm, the legal limitations and the cost and availability of credit.

1.8   INSTITUTIONAL FINANCE FOR EXPORT

Pre-shipment Credit:

Pre-shipment finance, also known as packing credit, refers to the credit extended to the exporter's prier to the shipment of goods. Pre-shipment credit enables an exporter to meet

a)   Working capital requirements for the purchase of raw materials and components,

b)   Processing packing,

c)   Transportation, warehousing, etc.,

d)   Packing credit is short-term finance.

"Packing Credit" is the term used for the pre-shipment short-term finance obtained by an exporter through his bankers. A loan is granted to him by the bankers with the view to financing his manufacturing activity exclusively in relation to specific export order/contracts.

Application to the Bank:

In order to avail packing credit, an exporter has to make a formal application to his bank either in a specified format or make an application, depending on the requirement imposed by the bank. Along with the application, a Firm contract with the buyer or export order and Letter of Credit received against the contract, should be enclosed.

Post-shipment Credit:

Most exporters do not position to extend credit to overseas buyers. To promote the export business, the burden of credit should be shifted from the exporters by either the financial institutions providing credit, directly or indirectly, to the buyers or by extending credit to their buyers. Accordingly, financial institutions provide buyer's credit, and supplier's credit.

Supplier's Credit.

Under the Buyer's Credit System, credit is extended to overseas buyer to pay for the goods he imports. If the financial institution that provides the buyer's credit is located in the exporter's country, the loan does not involve a transfer of funds from the supplier's country to the buyer's country; the exporter may obtain the payment directly from the financial institution of the relevant export documents. Buyer's credit is given in advance for capital goods.

Line of Credit:

When a number of buyers are involved, instead of negotiating credits with each one, the financial institutions in the supplier's country may extend a line of credit to a financial institution in the buyer's country which, in turn, will disburse the credit to the buyers in respect of approval transactions.

Short-term Finance:

Short term post-shipment credit is provided by the commercial banks, mainly by negotiating documents under letters of credit, by purchasing D/P and D/A bills, by lending against export bills tendered for collection abroad and by advancing money against such receivables as export incentives like cash assistance, refund of exercise and customs duty and reimbursement of the differentials between indigenous and international prices of certain raw material.

Medium and Long-term Finance:

The Industrial Development Bank of India (IDBI) played a very important role in long-term post-shipment finance. It provided refinance facilities to commercial banks against the long-term export credit extended by them, and had a scheme for direct financial assistance to exporters in collaboration with approved commercial banks.

1.9   EXPORT PROCEDURES INVOLVED IN INTERNATIONAL MARKETS:

Export Procedure activities are classified into five stages,

1. Preliminaries
2. Offer and receipt of confirmed orders
3. Production and clearance of the products for exports

4.   Shipment

5.   Negotiation of documents and realization of export proceeds and

6.   Obtaining various export incentives.

1) Preliminaries:

a) Importer-Exporter Code Number (IEC Number)

Individuals and business firms intending to export and or import goods and/or services should obtain an Importer-Exporter Number from the regional licensing authorities, unless exempted by DGFT. This number mentioned is to be shown in documents.

b) Membership in Certain Bodies:

After obtaining the IEC number, the exporters and importers may obtain membership in certain bodies like Export promotion Councils, India Trade promotion organization, etc., Membership in these organizations, help the exporter and importer regarding information and documentation.

c) Registration:

The exporter/importer has to register themselves with the Export promotion Councils (EPC), sales tax authorities, etc,

2) Inquiry, Offer and Receipt of Confirmed Order:

Inquiry is the request made by a prospective importer regarding his wish to improve certain goods, offer is a proposal submitted by an exporter expressing his intention to export specific goods at a specific terms and conditions. Exporter usually makes an offer in the form of a proforma invoice.'

The Proforma invoice includes the following items:

a) Name of the Buyer:

The complete name and address of the buyer/importer.

b) Description of Goods:

A brief description of goods indicating technical, Physical and chemical features. If necessary a detailed description is provided.

c) Price:

Unit wise and total price of the goods in interminiually accepted services or mutually agreed currencies. It should also cover the quantity discounts and cash discounts both in unit wise and total. The Price indicated in the invoice should be F.O.B and C.I.F or in other internationally accepted form.

d) Conditions of Sale:

Conditions of sale should be incorporated in details. Important among them are:

i) Validity:

The period for which to invoice is valid. The importer can accept the invoice any time before the validity period.

ii) Escalation clause:

The prices of the product may increase before the delivery period due to increase in the cost of inputs and thus the cost of production. Therefore, the exporter may include an escalation clause for escalation of price.

iii) Delivery Schedule:

A realistic delivery schedule is indicated. Based on the pricing mode, the exporter has to indicate the delivery schedule incase of C.I.F. quotations, the goods have to be delivered to the port of destination.

iv) Inspection:

The authority who will conduct inspection of goods, (if necessary) should also indicate.

v) Payment terms:

Payment terms like letter of credit, bill of exchange etc. should be included.

vi) Other obligations:

Other obligations of the following nature should also be included:

- Post sales service to be provided by the exporter.
- Providing spare parts.
- Warranty / guarantee for the equipment / technology.

vii)   Export License:

The exporter has to obtain the export license from the authorities concerned, if the items to be exported require a license.

viii)   Procuring finance:

If the exporter does not have the required finance to undertake the exports, he/she should obtain finance from different source.

3) Production / Procurement of Goods:

The exporting house after obtaining a confirmed order should produce the goods exactly as specified in the invoice. If the exporting house does not have production facilities, it has to procure the products from others.

4) Shipment:

Transporting the goods by ship is cheaper compared to that by air. In addition, physical size of the products creates hurdles for transporting by air.

Regarding shipment, the exporter has to contact shipping companies for space. After getting the confirmed order, sometimes, getting the space in ships is easy through agents as they have information of all shipping companies throughout the world.

The shipping company may issue shipping advice; the shipping company has no obligation to accept the cargo as the shipping advice is only providing information of availability of space at the time of issue of the acceptance. But in case of shipping order the shipping company has the obligation to accept the cargo.

a) Customs Clearance:

The exporter has to get custom clearance of the goods before; they are loaded on the ship. Customs authorities accord their formal approval after scrutinizing complete set of shipping documents, copies of shipping bill, etc. these documents include:

- Proforma invoice in original and duplicate
- GR-I form (in duplicate)
- AR-4 form (in original and duplicate)
- Export License (if required)

- Letter of credit covering the export order, export contract or order in original
- Certificate of inspection (Where necessary)
- Form of declaration (in duplicate)
- Shipping bill (five copies)
- Quality control Inspection Certificate (if required)
- Original contract wherever available
- Packing list
- Letter of Registration Certificate (if applicable)

b) GR-I Form:

This form is an exchange control document required by the Reserve Bank of India. The exporter has to realize the proceeds of the goods exported within 130 days from the date of the shipment from India. This form is not necessary in case of export of Nepal and Bhutan.

c) Shipping Bill:

This is an exchanged document needed by the customs officials for granting permission for shipment. This bill contains the following information.

- Name of the Exporter / shipper including his address and IEC number.
- Description and quantity of goods to be shipped.
- Value of goods.
- Number of packages and markings on them.
- Amount of drawback (drawback duty is allowed when the goods are produced in India)
- Port of destination
- Names of the ship and its agent

Five copies of the shipping bill are to be provided to the custom officials.

d) Export License:

Export license is necessary for certain categories of goods. Export license can be obtained from the Joint Director General of Foreign Trade (JDGFT).

e) Carting Order

The superintendent of the Port Trust issues the order called carting order for moving the goods in to the port area after verifying the shipping bill and shipping order.

f) Let Ship:

After getting the approval from the customs officials, the exporter arranges for loading the products on the ship. Before loading takes place, the exporter's forwarding agent has to get the permission from the preventive officer of the customs department. This permission is called the 'Let Ship Order'.

h) Port Trust Dues:

The Port Trust, Authorities after receiving the 'Mate's Receipt', from the captain of the ship, issues the 'bill of lading' to the exporter.

I) Bill of lading:

The Exporter's forwarding agent collects the 'Mates Receipt' and submits the same to the authorities and in turn collects the bill of lading from the port authorities.

The exporter's forwarding agent provides the following documents to the exporter at the final stage they are:

- A copy of the invoice duty attested by the customs
- Drawback copy of the shipping bill
- Export promotion copy of the shipping bill
- Full set of 'clean on board' bill of lading together with the non-negotiable copies
- The original letter of the credit
- Customer's order or contract
- Duplicate copy of the AR-4 form

j) Shipping by other modes of transport:

All the goods are not transported through ship. Other modes of transport like air and land are also used for exporting the goods.

The goods which are of less weight and perishable and are required urgently by the importer are transported by air.

Shipping by Posts certain goods of less weight are exported by post. The emergence of one laid down for export by sea. AR-4 form is different for export by land. The excisable goods are presented to the Frontier Customs Officer.

Shipping by Land: Export of the excisable goods to the nearby countries is similar to the one laid down for export by sea. AR-4 form is different for export by land. The excisable goods are presented to the frontier Customs Office/Border Examiner along with form 4A.

5. Documents:

The exporter submits the relevant documents to his banker for getting the payment for the goods exported. Submission of relevant documents to the bank is called "Negotiating the Documents", through the bank. These documents are called 'Negotiable Set of Documents', this set normally includes.

- Bill of lading
- Commercial Invoice together with the packing slip and bill of exchange
- Certificate of origin
- GR-I for (in duplicate)
- Marine Insurance Policy (in duplicate)
- Letter of credit (in original)

6. Export Incentives:

Export incentives include:

- **Duty Drawback:**

Exporter is eligible to get back the excise duty and central excise paid on all raw materials, components and consumables used in the production of goods exported, under this scheme.

- **Excise Duty Refund:**

Exporter is eligible for refund of the excise duty. He/She can recover it after export, if he paid at the beginning. He/She also can execute a bond with the Excise authorities without making the payment.

The Policy regarding export from the country is formulated by the Director General of Foreign Trade, Government of India, Ministry of

Commerce, and New Delhi. While the physical movement of goods exported is regulated by the Customs Authorities, the Reserve Bank of India, Exchange Control Department, in terms of the relevant provision of the Foreign Exchanged Regulation Act, it is concerned about the realization and realization and repatriation of export proceeds to India within the prescribed period and in the prescribed manner. For further details and clarifications, exporters are advised to refer to the Exchange Control Manual (1993 Edition) as amended from time to time and/or approach any Office of the Reserve Bank or Authorized Dealers (Banks).

EXPORT DECLARATION FORMS

In terms of Sec. 18 of the Foreign Exchange Regulation Act (FERA) 1973 and Rule 5 of the Foreign Exchange Regulation Rules, 1974, every exporter must declare to the prescribed authority in the prescribed form the full export value of the goods that are exported to any place outside India other than Nepal and Bhutan. The forms contain an undertaking that the exporter will deliver to the Bank named in the form, the Foreign Exchange representing the full export value of the goods on or before the due data for payment or six months from the date of shipment whichever is earlier in the manner prescribed in Rule 9 of the Foreign Rules, 1974. This is a legally binding one and failure to fulfill it would attract the penal provisions of FERA, 1973. The Export Declaration Forms act as a vital link between the agencies (Customs/Post Offices) under whose supervision goods leave India and the agencies (Authorized Dealers and the Reserve Bank of India) which monitor the realization of Foreign Exchange proceeds of the exported goods.

Types of Export Declaration Forms

At present there are four types of Export Declaration Forms in use. All Exports, other than the ones exempt from declaration, must be declared on an appropriate form as indicated below:

a)   GR Form is used for export to all countries made otherwise than by Post.

b)   PP Form is used for exports to all countries by Parcel Post.

c)   VP/COD Form is used for exports to all countries by Parcel Post under Arrangements to realize proceeds through Postal channels on a 'value Payable' or cash on delivery' basis.

d)   SOFTEX Form is used in the place of GR Form when computer software is exported in the non-physical Form'

The Export Declaration Forms are printed by the RBI. The forms bear printed serial numbers.

Exempted Exports

Certain categories of exports are exempt from declaration. The exemptions which are made for serving the general public are:

i)   Goods dispatched by Air freight or Post Parcels, provide the packet is accompanied by a Declaration by the sender that the value of the goods is not more than Rs.10,000 and the export does not involve any transaction in Foreign Exchange.

ii)   Goods dispatched by Air Freight or Post Parcel, where the Parcel is accompanied by a Certificate issued by an Authorized Dealer (AD) that the export of goods does not involve any transaction in Foreign Exchange. The AD will issue his Certificate provided inter alia the following conditions are fulfilled.

a)   The sender is a regular customer of the AD and the customer makes an Application for the Certificate.

b)   The AD is satisfied that the export does not involve any transaction in Foreign Exchange and

c)   The Value of the shipment does not exceed Rs.25, 000.

The Certificate issued by the AD will also carry a notation to the effect that the value of the Shipment should be subject to acceptance by Customs.

FOREIGN EXCHANGE FACILITIES:

The following Foreign Exchange facilities are available to the exporters as per RBI's new Exchange Control Manual, 1993 Edition.

The Agents/Consignees may deduct from sale proceeds of the goods, expense normally incurred towards receipt, storage and sale of the goods, such as landing charges, warehouse rent, handling charges etc., and remit the net proceeds to the exporter. Foreign Exchange is released/remitted abroad freely Currency Accounts known as EEFC accounts and FCA in India and/or abroad even. Foreign Exchange facilities thus cover.

1. Foreign Currency Accounts
2. Foreign Travel
3. Agency Commission
4. Export Claims
5. Reduction in Export Invoice Value
6. Expenses on Dishonored Export Bills
7. Arbitration Fee
8. Publicity and Advertisement
9. Newspapers and Magazines/Journals Subscription
10. Membership fee for Trade Associations
11. Testing Charges
12. Overseas Branches/Offices
13. Tender Documents
14. Export Information
15. Trade Samples
16. Exploration of Foreign Markets
17. Fairs/Exhibitions Abroad
18. Hospitality to Non-resident-Visitors
19. Engagement of Foreign Technician(s)
20. Patent, Trade Mark Fees
21. Registration Fee for Conferences
22. Maintenance/Annual Service Charges for Machinery/ Software
23. Replacement of Parts/articles
24. Freight Payment in Foreign Currency
25. Electronic Database Costs
26. Legal Expenses Connected with exports
27. Consultancy Fees
28. Feasibility/Pre-feasibility Studies for Projects in India
29. Miscellaneous Remittances and
30. Miscellaneous Purposes

Chapter-II

2.1 FOREIGN EXCHANGE REGULATIONS AND FORMALITIES

MEANING:

"Foreign exchange is the system or process of converting one national currency into another, and of transferring money from one country to another". (Dr Paul Einzing).

The term foreign exchange is used to refer to foreign currencies, the Foreign Exchange Regulation Act, 1973 (FERA), defines foreign exchange as foreign currency and includes all deposits, credits and balance payable in any foreign currency and any drafts, travelers' cheques, letters of credits and bills of exchange, expressed or drawn in Indian currency, but payable in any foreign currency.

The importing country pays money to the exporting country in return of goods either in its domestic currency or the hard currency. This currency which facilitates the payment to complete the transaction is called Foreign Exchange.

This foreign exchange is the money in one country for money or credit or goods of services in another country. Foreign exchange includes foreign exchange markets. The components of foreign exchange market include the buyers, the sellers and the intermediaries. Foreign exchange market is not restricted to any place or country. In fact, foreign exchange in recent times is traded through on-line (internet). Foreign exchange market is the market for currencies of various countries anywhere in the globe. As the financial centers of the world are united as a single market.

The market intermediaries of foreign exchange market include:

- **Exchange Banks dealing in foreign exchange** These banks discount and sell foreign bills of exchange, issue bank drafts, effect travelers' cheques and telegraphic transfers.

- **Bill brokers:**   They help sellers and buyers to come together.

- **Acceptance houses:**   They help sellers and buyers to come together.

- **Central Bank of the country:**   It also deals in foreign exchange.

Foreign Exchange Market:

The Foreign exchange market is a market in which foreign exchange transactions take place. In other words a foreign exchange market is a market in which national currencies are bought and sold against one another.

The five main levels of foreign exchange business dealings are:

- Transactions between banks and non-bank customers.

- Transactions between banks dealing in foreign exchange in the same market.

- Transactions between banks dealing in foreign exchanges in different centers.

- Transactions between banks dealing in foreign exchange and the central banks in the same country; and

- Transactions in foreign exchanges between central banks of different countries.

Functions of Foreign Exchange Market:

A foreign exchange market performs the following there important function.

Transfer of Purchasing Power:

The Primary function of a foreign exchange market is the transfer of purchasing power from one country to another and from one currency to another. The international clearing function performed by the foreign exchange markets plays a very important role in facilitation international trade and capital movements.

Provision of Credit:

The credit function performed by foreign exchange markets plays a very important role n the growth of foreign trade, for international trade depends to a great extent on credit facilities. Exporters may get pre-shipment and post-shipment credit. Credit facilities are available also for importers.

Provision of Hedging Facilities:

The other important function of the foreign exchange market is to provide hedging facilities, Hedging refers to the coverage of export risks. It provides a mechanism by which exporters and importers may guard themselves against the losses arising from fluctuations in exchange rates.

2.2 KINDS OF EXCHANGE RATE:

The important types of transactions involved in the foreign exchange market are:

Spot and Forward Exchange Rates:

The term spot exchange refers to the class of foreign exchange transactions which require the delivery exchange, of currencies on the spot. In practice, the settlement takes place within two days in most markets. The rate of exchange effective for spot sanction is known as the spot market.

The forward transaction is an agreement between two parties. Requiring the delivery at some specified future date of a specified amount of foreign currency by one of the parties against payment in domestic currency by the other party at the price agreed upon in the contract. The rate of exchange applicable to the forward contract is called the forward exchange rate.

The foreign exchange regulations of various countries generally regulate the forward exchange transactions with a view to curbing speculation in foreign currencies. In India, commercial banks are permitted to offer forward cover only in respect of genuine export and import transactions.

Forward Exchange Rates:

With reference to its relationship with the spot rate, the forward rate may be at par, at discount or at a premium.

At Par:

If the forward exchange rate quoted is exactly equivalent to the spot rate at the time of making the contract. Forward exchange rate is said to be at par.

At Premium:

The forward rate for a currency any. The US dollar is said to be at a premium, with respect to the spot rate when one dollar buys more units of another currency, say the rupee, in the forward rather than in the spot market.

At Discount:

The forward exchange rate is determined mostly by the demand for, and supply of, Forward exchange naturally. When the demand for forward exchange exceeds its supply the forward rate will be quoted at a premium.

When the supply of forward exchange exceeds the demand for it, the rate will be quoted at a discount. When the supply is equivalent to the demand for forward exchange, the forward rate will tend to be at par.

Multiple rates:

If a country adopts more than one rate of exchange for its currency. It is said to follow a system of multiple exchange rates. It may have one rate for exports and another for imports: or it may have one rate of exchange (viz. controlled rate) with some countries, and another rate (viz. free exchange rates) with others.

Two tire exchange rate system:

A form of multiple exchange rates is known as the two-tier exchange rate system under which the government maintains two rates – a higher rate for commercial transactions and lower rate for capital transactions. Since 1971, France and Italy have adopted this system.

Arbitrage:

Arbitrage is the act of simultaneously buying a currency in one market and selling it in another market to make a profit by taking advantage of price or exchange rate differences in the two markets. If the arbitrage operations are confined to two markets only, they will be known as 'two point arbitrage' If they extend to three to more markets they are known as 'three point' or multi point' arbitrage.

Swap operation:

Commercial banks who conduct forward exchange business may resort to a swap operation to adjust their fund position. The term swap means simultaneous sale of spot currency for the forward purchase of the same currency or purchase of spot for the forward sale of the same currency. The Spot is swapped against forward. Operations consisting of a simultaneous sale or purchase of spot currency accompanied by a purchase or sale respectively of the same currency of forward delivery, are technically known as swaps or double deals, as the spot currency is swapped against forward.

EXCHANGE RATE DETERMINATION:

The transactions in the foreign exchange market, viz., buying and selling foreign currency take at a rate, is called 'exchange rate'. Exchange rate is the price in the home currency for a unit of foreign currency. The exchange rate can be quoted in two ways.

- One unit of foreign money to a number of units of domestic currency.

- A certain number of Units of foreign currency to one unit of domestic currency.

For example: I US $=50 or Re. I=I US $ 0.02.

Exchange rate in a free market is determined by the demand for and the supply of exchange of a particular country. The equilibrium exchange rate at which demand for foreign exchange and the supply of foreign exchange are equal.

1. Demand of Foreign Exchange:

The demand for foreign exchange is determined by the country's:

- Import of goods and services.

- Investment in foreign countries (flow of capital to other countries) i.e. establishment of an industry by Indian in USA.

- Other payments involved in international transactions like payments of Indian Government to various foreign governments for settlement of their transactions.

- Other types of outflow of foreign capital like giving donations etc.

2. Supply of Foreign Exchange:

Supply of Foreign exchange of a particular country (i.e. US dollars) indicates the availability of foreign currency of a particular country concerned (i.e.India) in its foreign exchange market. The supply of foreign exchange includes:

- Country's exports of goods and services to foreign countries
- Inflow of foreign capital
- Payments made by the foreign governments to Indian government for selling their transactions.
- Other types of inflow of foreign capital like remittances by the Non-Resident Indians, donations received etc.,

2.3   SYSTEMS OF EXCHANGE RATES:

FIXED EXCHANGE RATES:

The maintenance of stable rate of exchange has been the major monetary objective of all countries. The International Monetary Fund (IMF) was established with the objective of stabilizing the rates of exchanges. Under fixed or pegged exchange rates all exchange transactions take place at an exchange rate that is determined by the monetary authority. The system of fixed change came to be known as pegged exchange rates or par values.

Fixed exchange rate refers to the system under which the rate of exchange of a currency is fixed or pegged in terms of gold or in terms of another currency. In other words, countries following the fixed change rate (also known as stable exchange rate and pegged exchange rate) system agree to keep their currencies at a fixed, pegged rate and to change their value only at fairly infrequent intervals. When the economic situation forces them to do so.

MERITS:

1) Smooth flow of international trade:

International trade will flow more quickly and more easily when there is confidence all round that the existing rate will continue in future.

2) International investment:

International investment will be promoted through a system of stable exchange rates.

3) Remove speculation:

Stable exchange rate will remove the dangerous possibilities of speculation. For, past experience with fluctuating exchange rates has shown that movements in the rate of exchange are significantly affected by large transfer of capital.

4) Less inflationary:

It leads to greater monetary discipline and so to less inflationary pressure.

DEMERITS:

The following are the demerits of fixed exchange rates:

1. Sacrifice of objectives:

The fixed change rates is the sacrifice of the objectives of full employment and stable price at the alter of stable exchange rates. This is bound to impose large social costs within the country.

2. Heavy burden:

Under it large reserves of foreign currencies are required to be maintained. Countries with balance of payment deficit must have large reserves if they want to avoid devaluation. If countries wish to remain on the fixed exchange rates system, they must hold large reserves of foreign currencies. This also imposes a heavy burden on the monetary authority for managing foreign exchange reserves.

3. Mal allocation of resources:

This system requires complicated exchange of control measures which lead to mal allocation of the company's resources.

4. Dependence in international institutions:

Under this system, a country mostly depends upon international institutions for borrowing and lending foreign currencies.

5. Balance of payment disequilibrium:

It fails to solve the problem of balance of payment disequilibrium. This is difficult to be tacked because of monetary, fiscal and other measures.

FLEXIBLE EXCHANGE RATES:

Under flexible exchange rate is system exchange rate if freely determined in an open market primarily by private dealings, and, like other market prices, vary from day - to day.

Floating rate of exchange comes into existence when the currency unit of a country is free to fluctuate and find its own level, according to conditions of demand and supply in the foreign exchange market.

MERITS:

1) Promotes of international trade:

So long as traders have confidence, in the existing exchange rates and in the ability of the government to maintain them, there will no difficult and the flow of international trade will be smooth. Under this system, the importer or exporter need not be afraid of fluctuation exchange rates because he can always protect himself through the system of forward exchange rates.

2) Promotion of International investment:

Under the system, neither the borrower nor the lender can surely expect that the exchange rate in which he is interested will remain stable fore decades. Therefore, the long term loan floated for development purposes will be favorably influenced by the system of fixed exchange rates, but adversely influenced by flexible exchange rates is not valid.

3) Currency area:

It is pointed out that stable exchange rates are not really necessary for any system of currency areas. Certain economic, political and social forces have bound the various countries to form the sterling block and these forces would not be weakened if the sterling is allowed to have flexible exchange, after consultation among member – countries of the block.

4) Prevent speculation:

The chief defect of the stable exchange rates is that it encourages currency speculation, which will definitely destroy and make devaluation of the currency inevitable. A second disability of a stable exchange rate is that too often the rate does not reflect the existing and true cost price relationship between two countries.

5) Need not to borrow and lend short term funds:

When foreign exchange rates move freely, there is no need to have international institutional arrangements like the IMF for borrowing and lending short term funds to remove disequilibrium in the balance of payments.

DEMERITS:

1) Mal allocation of resources:

The main disadvantage is that it would bring about an appropriate exchange rate. The equilibrium exchange rate in the foreign exchange market at a point of time may not give correct signals to concerned parties in the country. This may lead to wrong decisions and mal allocation of resources with the country.

2) No justification for the government:

As a corollary, There is no justification for a government to leave the determination of exchange rates to international market forces when price, rents, wages, interest rates etc., are often controlled by the government.

3) Encouragement to inflation:

This system has inflationary bias. A system of flexible exchange rates, a depreciation of the exchange rate leads to a dangerous position of inflation. Depreciation leads to a rise in   prices thereby making import goods more expensive. This lead to cost push inflation.

4) Crashes the world market:

This exchange system crashes up the world market. There is no one's money which serves as a medium of exchange, unit of account, store of value and a standard of deferred payment. Under it, the world market for goods and capital would be divided. Resources allocation would be vastly sub-optimal.

5) BALANCE OF PAYMENT DEFICIT IS NOT SOLVED:

Under developed countries faces the problem of deficit in their balance of payments because they import raw materials, machinery, capital equipments, etc. for their development. But their exports are limited to primary and other products which fetch low prices in world markets.

This balance of payments deficit can be removed in a system of flexible exchange rates.

2.4   PRE-SHIPMENT STAGE

Pre-shipment stage consists of the following steps.

a) Approaching Foreign Buyers:

Usually exporters approach foreign buyers by techniques such as international media, sales promotion, Public relation, personal selling, Publicity and participation in trade fairs and exhibitions.

b) Inquiry and offer:

An inquiry is a request from a prospective importer about description of goods, their standard or grade. Size, weight or quantity, terms of payments, etc., on getting an inquiry, the exporter must process an immediately by making an offer in the form of a Performa invoice.

C) CONFIRMATION OF ORDER:

Once the negotiations are completed and the terms and conditions are finished the exporter send three copies of Performa Invoice to the importer for the confirmation of order. The importer signs these copies and sends back two copies to the exporter.

d) Opening Letter of Credit:

The documentary credit or letter of credit is the most appropriate and secured method of payment adopted to settle international transactions. On finalization of the export Contract the importer open a letter of credit in favour of the exporter, if agreed upon in the contract.

e) Arrangement of pre-shipment Finance:

On securing the letter of credit, the exporter procures pre-shipment finance from his bank for procuring raw materials and other components, processing and packing of goods and transfer of goods to the port of shipment.

f) Production or-Procurement of Goods:

One securing the pre-shipment finance from the bank, the exporter either arranges for the production of the required goods, or procures them from the domestic market as per the specifications of the importer.

g) Packing and Marketing:

Then the goods should be properly packed and marked with necessary details such as port of shipment and destination, country of origin, gross and net weight, etc. If required, assistance can be taken from the Indian Institute of packing (IIP).

h) Pre-shipment 'Inspection:

If the goods to be exported are subject to compulsory quality control and pre-shipment inspection then exporter should contact the Export Inspection Agency (EIA) for obtaining an inspection certificate.

i) Central Excise Clearance:

The exporters are totally exempted from the payment of central excise duty. However, the exemption should be claimed in one of the following ways:

- Export under Rebate
- Export under bond

j) Obtaining Insurance Cover:

The exporter must take appropriate policies in order to insure risks.

ECGE Policy in order to cover credit risks.

- Marine Policy, if the price quotation agreed upon is CIF.

k) Appointment of C&F Agent:

Since exporting is a complex and time consuming process, the exporter should appoint a clearing and forwarding (C&F) agent for the smooth clearance of goods from the customs and preparation and submission of various export documents.

2.5   MARKET INTELLIGENCE AND MARKET RESEARCH INFORMATION REQUIRED FOR EXPORTS:

The information requirement for exports is the following:

1. International Business Decision Related Information:

There information about the prospects of the foreign markets, competition, other characteristics prospects of the foreign market, domestic market prospects, etc., is required to make international business.

2. Market Selection Related Information:

The market related factors are political and economic stability, currency stability, government policy and regulation, etc. Market selection also requires specific information about the product or industry concerned such as the demand trends, Government policy and regulation, competitive situation, etc.

3. Product Related Information:

Like consumer tastes and preferences about the product like unit, size, quantity, shape, colour, product form, packaging, etc.; mode, time, frequencies and rates of consumption; purpose of use, uses, etc; regulatory aspects and so on are needed.

4. Price Related Information:

Price related information is prevailing price ranges, price trends, margins, pricing, practices, government polices and regulations, price elasticity of demand, role of price as a strategic marketing variable, etc.

5. Price Related Information:

Promotion related aspects such as media availability and effectiveness, government regulations, customs/practices of promotion in the market concerned, competitive behaviour. etc., are vital.

6. Distribution Related Information:

Distribution Related Information includes information on factors such as channel alternatives and characteristics, relative effectiveness of different channels, customs and practices of the trade, power and influence of channel members, etc.

7. *Competition Related Information:*

A company will also need information about the competitive environment, including the extent of competition, major competitors, relative strengths and weaknesses of competitors, strategies and behaviour of competitors, etc. to make decisions relating to exports.

MARKETING INFORMATION SYSTEM AND MARKETING RESEARCH

According to Terpstra : "International marketing intelligence involves the creation of an information system, which should, of course, be a part of the company's overall information system for international business. Viewed from this perspective, international marketing intelligence includes several different tasks, one of which is marketing research on individual foreign markets."2

The Committee on Definitions of the American Marketing Association defines marketing research as "The systematic gathering, recording, and analyzing of data about problem relating to the marketing of goods and services."

A modified definition is that marketing research is "the systematic planning, gathering, recording, analyzing and interpreting of data for application to specific marketing decisions."3   This modified definition adds two more stages, namely, planning and interpreting, and states that marketing research is meant to help decision making.

Marketing Information System is defined as "an interacting, continuing, future-oriented structure of people, equipment and procedures. It is designed to generate and process an information flow to aid decision making in a company's marketing program."4

Objectives of Marketing Research:

Marketing research is very important to keep pace with the changing environment characterized by

(a) Increasing competition;

(b) Fast technological development;

(c) Changing consumer attitudes;

(d) Changing tastes and requirements.

The basic use of marketing research is that it helps the company to indentify the problem areas and environmental opportunities and helps monitor the environment. One may list several benefits of marketing research, but all these converge to what has been stated earlier. Thus marketing research helps to:

1.   Identify the deficiencies, of the,
   a)   Products
   b)   Pricing
   c)   Distribution
   d)   Promotion
2.   Identify existing and emerging marketing opportunities
3.   Identify the relative weaknesses and strength of the company.
4.   Monitor the environmental changes.

Limitations of Marketing Research

1.   Research findings are not always entirely dependable. The performance of may products have been in contrast to the research indications.
2.   Research involves costs, and the cost can, at times, be formidable.
3.   Non-availability of adequate and reliable data, problems in collecting data (including the problems caused by social attitudes, deficiencies of research agencies and in house research facilities.
4.   It is a time-consuming process.

Scope of Marketing Research

The scope of marketing research is very wide. The broad areas of research are:

1.   Product research
2.   Pricing research
3.   Distribution research
4.   Promotion research
5.   Consumer research
6.   Marketing environment research

7.   Market trend research

8.   Marketing efficiency research

TYPES OF RESEARCH

Broadly, there are two types of research, viz.

i)   Exploratory research

ii) Conclusive research

Exploratory Research

"Exploratory research seeks to discover new relationships, while conclusive research is designed to help executives choose among the possible course of action, i.e., to make decisions."5

Exploratory research is investigative in nature. For example, the problem may be to find out why the sales of a product are poor or why a particular group of consumers likes or dislikes the product.

"Exploratory research may define a problem which is then 'solved' by conclusive research, but conclusive research may have by-products which are, in effect, new exploratory studies leading to new hypothesis."

An exploratory research may be conducted by:

i)   Study of secondary data

ii) Survey of knowledgeable persons

iii) Analysis of selected cases, i.e., intensive study of a relatively small number of situations.

Conclusive Research

There are two types of conclusive research, namely

i)   Descriptive research

ii) Experimental research

Descriptive studies are designed to describe certain things (for example, the characteristics of users of a given product; the degree to which product use varies with demographic variables such as age, sex, income, etc.)

Descriptive research may be conducted by:

i)   Case study

ii)   Statistical study

The statistical method differs from the case method in the number of cases studied and in the comprehensiveness of the study of each case. While the case method involves a complete study of a few cases, statiscal method involves the study of few factors in a large number of cases".

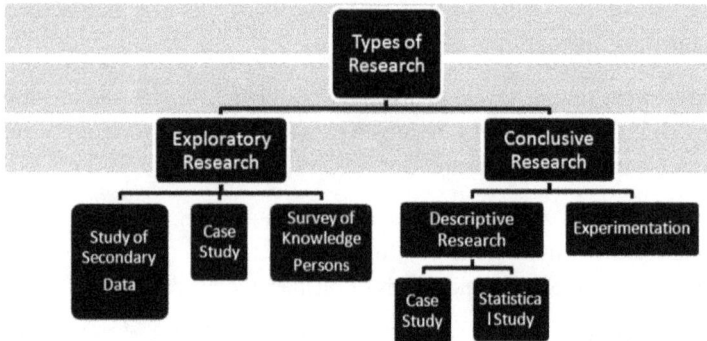

PHASES OF A RESEARCH PROJECT

The important steps involved in carrying out research are as follows:

1)   Definition of the problem

2)   Conducting of a situational analysis

3)   Conducting of an informal study

4)   Formulation of the research design

5)   Collection of information

6)   Analysis and interpretation of data

7)   Presentation of research findings

1) Definition of the Problem:

The first step in the marketing research project is definition of the research proble, i.e. the objective or purpose of the research study should be clearly laid down. Helps it collect the required information, avoid gathering irrelevant information, analyze and interpret data in the proper perspective and to make the best use of the time and other resources.

2) *Situational Analysis:*

Situational analysis is important when marketing research is conducted by an outside agency the situational analysis is meant to familiarize the researcher with the company and its environmentand thereby makethe problem more clearly to the researcher.

3) *Informal Investigation:*

This step is an extension of the previous step. While the situational analysis is largely confined to information from company sources in this stage, the researcher gathers more information from external sources such as competitors, middlemen, advertising agencies, customers, etc.

4) *Research Design:*

A research design is the specification of methods and procedures for acquiring the information needed. It is the overall operational pattern or framework of the project that stipulates what information is to be collected from which sources and by what procedures. If it is a good research design, it will ensure that the information obtained is relevant to the questions, and that it was collected by objective and economical procedures."[8]

A research design, thus, specifies:

i) The type of information required

ii) The sources of the information

iii) The methods or techniques of data collection

Broadly, there are two sources of information, viz.

i) Secondary sources

ii) Primary sources

Secondary and Primary Data:

Secondary data are data which have already been gathered by somebody else and available to others for use. Such data may be available in published or unpublished form. Books, journals, periodicals, newspapers, reports, theses, dissertations, term papers, papers presented in seminars and symposia, etc., are sources of secondary data.

Primary data are first-hand data collected by the research. Sometimes primary data may be unreliable.

Collection of Data:

The research design specifies the data requirements, sources of data, methods of data collection and the sampling technique and the sample size. After these things have been specified, it may be necessary to prepare data collection forms like questionnaires/schedules. It may also be necessary to pre-test the questionnaire before data collection starts in real earnest to ensure that the questions are clear and do not cause embarrassment to the respondents.

Processing, Analysis and Interpretation Data:

The raw data have to be processed and presented in an appropriate form like tables to make them easily amenable to analysis. Analysis should be followed by interpretation which includes expressing the findings in more meaningful terms like percentage and drawing useful inferences from them.

Presentation of Findings:

The research findings should be presented in any appropriate form (like a report, for example). The type of presentation to be made depends on a number of factors like the nature of research, its purpose and use, the persons who use them, etc. The findings should be presented in a form and language that will be easily understood by the people who use them.

METHODS OF DATA COLLECTION

For collecting primary data, there are broadly two methods, viz.

   i)   Observation

   ii)   Survey

Observational Research

This is the method of collecting data by observing the behaviour of people in a given situation. The observation may be carried out in a natural situation. For example, the response of consumers to a particular display may be observed in an actual store. An alternative is to observe the consumer behaviour in a simulated situation. For example, a mocking store may be established to observe the consumer behaviour.

The observation may be made openly or through hidden cameras, one-way mirrors or by disguised observers.

The observational method is helpful to collect information that people are unwilling or unable to provide.

Merits the merits of the observational method are:

i) It provides information about the actual behaviour of consumers.

ii) Chances of bias are limited.

iii) It helps obtain information which consumers are unwilling or unable to provide.

Limitations:

The limitations of the observational method are:

i) It is helpful in getting information only about certain aspects of consumer behaviour.

ii) It provides information only about how consumers behave; it does not provide any information as to why consumers behave so.

iii) In most cases, it is useful only as a supplement to other methods.

Survey Research

This method enables collection of information directly from the consumers. The important contact methods used to collect information by the survey method are:

i) Personal interviewing

ii) Telephone interviewing

iii) Mail questionnaires

Personal Interviewing

There are two forms of personal interviewing, viz.

a) Individual interviewing

b) Group interviewing

Individual interviewing

Individual interviewing is more suitable than group interviewing for collecting information that is too personal.

Group interviewing

Group interviewing is less costly than personal interviewing. Certain information which may not be readily forthcoming from individual interviewing may be forthcoming from group interviewing. In group interviewing, the respondents are likely to be more controlled than in individual interviewing. This has both positive and negative effects.

Merits:

The merits of personal interviewing are as under:

It is the most direct way of eliciting information from the respondents.

   i.   It is the most direct way of eliciting information from the respondents,

   ii. It enables the researcher to take the respondent into confidence so as to get his full co-operation.

   iii. It enables clarification of points,

   iv. It enables the cross-checking of the information provided,

   v.   It also provides for certain flexibility needed for data collection,

   vi. It enables the investigator to observe the environment of the respondent,

Limitations:

The important limitations of personal interviewing are as under:

   i)   It is time-consuming and costly, particulary if the respondents are large in number and widely scattered.

   ii) Some respondents may be hesitant to reveal certain information in a face-to-face interview.

   iii) This method needs trained people who are tactful in collecting information.

Telephone Interviewing:

Telephone interviewing is an easy method of collecting information. It is very common in advanced countries where most people are available on phone. In countries like India this method can be employed only in certain cases because of the limitations of telephone ownership. However, this can be employed when the sample consists of people of certain specific strata.

Merits:

Important merits of telephone interviewing are as under:

 i) Easy and quick method.

 ii) Like personal interviewing, this method also enables taking the respondent into confidence, clarification of points, cross-checking of information to some extent, etc.

 iii) As it avoids a face-to-face situation, it is a better method than personal interviewing to get certain types of information, like those which are very personal or sensitive.

 iv) It saves time and cost compared to personal interviewing.

Limitations:

Following are the important limitations of telephone interviewing:

 i) Its scope is limited in countries like India where most people are not available on the phone and where the telephone system is iefficient.

 ii) One limitation of this method in comparison with personal interviewing is that there is no scope for personally observing the respondent in his environment.

Mail Questionnaire:

One common method is to send the questionnaire to the respondent by post.

Merits:

Important merits of this method are as under:

 i) When the respondents are large in number and scattered over distant places, this is a preferable method.

 ii) It is also a very economical method.

 iii) Respondents can fill in the questionnaire at their leisure, and hence, they may be in a position to do justice to the requirements.

iv)   It avoids embarrassment of talking to a person about certain sensitive matters.

Limitations:

Limitation of the questionnaire method includes:

i)   It cannot be used to collect information from the illiterate.

ii)   It does not provide scope for clarification,

iii) It does not provide as much scope for cross-checking as in the case of personal or telephone interviewing.

iv)   There are chances of the respondents leaving some parts of the questionnaire blank.

v)   Many respondents may have to be reminded over and again to send back the questionnaire.

vi)   The response rate (i.e., the percentage of people who fill in properly and return the questionnaire) is normally very low.

SAMPLING:

When the size of the population, i.e., number of relevant units to be studied, is very large, sampling becomes necessary for conducting the market research. For example, certain consumer products like toilet soap or toothpaste have several crores of consumers and no market research can afford to make a survey of the entire population of consumers to study the consumer characteristics. A survey of a few hundred consumers selected in such a way as to possess the representative character of the relevant population will serve the purpose of marketing research.

It many market researches, information are collected from a representative sample and not from the entire population. When the relevant population is very small, it will be possible, and may be necessary, to adopt the census method or complete enumeration method, i.e., of studying all the units. In other cases, sampling may be resorted to.

Reasons for Sampling

1)   When the population size is very large, it is not possible to collect information about all the units within a limited time.

2)   When the population is very large, collection of information from all the units would be prohibitively expensive.

3)   Besides the two problems mentioned, there could be other practical difficulties like getting sufficient number of qualified investigators, locating all the units, etc.

4)   In most cases, a representative sample would provide reasonably adequate and accurate information and the accuracy of information is not going to be justifiably enhanced by studying the entire population.

5)   In certain situations, sampling is the only justifiable method. For example. if the material gets destroyed in the process of testing (Example: testing of photographic film), there will not be any useful material left after testing if the entire output is subjected to testing.

Sample Characteristics

A sample to be justifiable should possess the following qualities:

1)   It should be representative of the population so that the information collected from the sample will be dependable.

2)   The sample should be of adequate size to ensure reasonable accuracy of information.

3)   Sampling is justifiable in terms of time and other resources.

Limitation of Sampling

There may arise sampling error, i.e. the error in selecting the sample. If there is a sampling error, the sample will not be the true representative of the population.

The reliability of the sample depends on the appropriateness of the sampling method used.

Methods of Sampling

There are two broad categories of sampling, viz., non-probability sampling and probability sampling.

Non-Probability Sampling

The following are the important non-probability methods of sampling.

i) Convenience Sampling:

Units include in the sample are selected according to the convenience of the investigator. For example, for a sample survey of bus passengers, passengers waiting at bus stops may be included in the sample.

ii) Quota Control Sampling:

Under the quota control sampling, the field workers are required to include in the sample only those units which conform to certain specified parameters and each field worker is assigned quotas of number of units to include according to one or more characteristics. For example, the interviewer may be asked to include in the sample to bus passengers 20 male students, 15 female student, 30 male employees, 10 female employees and 25 other regular passengers.

iii) Judgment Sampling:

Under this method, units are included in the sample on the basis of the judgment that the units possess the required characteristics to qualify as representatives of the population. The judgment may be qualitative (an expert opinion) or quantitative (based on certain quantifiable characteristics).

Probability Sampling

There are a number of methods of probability sampling. Some important ones are given here.

i) Simple Random Sampling:

Units are selected at random so that every unit has an equal chance of getting included in the sample.

ii) Stratified Random Sampling:

When the relevant population consists of different strata like low-income households, lower-middle income households, upper-middle income households, high-income households, etc., the population is divided into different strata and certain specified number of units are selected from each stratum at random. It also involves decision about the weightage to be given to each stratum in the sample size.

iii) Systematic Sampling:

Under this method, every n-th unit is selected from the target population list after the first unit is selected at random.

iv) Cluster Sampling:

Under cluster sampling, a cluster of the relevant population is studied instead of individual units from a very wide area. For example, for a certain study, all the households in a particular neighbourhood (residential) of a city may be included in the sample rather than selecting one or a few households from every neighbourhood of the entire city.

PROBLEMS IN INTERNATIONAL RESEARCH:

The different problems in international business research are:

* The cultural differences   make foreign market research a difficult task.
* It is often very expensive.
* The research methodology suitable for one market may not be suitable for another market.

2.6   EXPORT PRICING

Introduction:

High Prices will combine with a high – quality image and must be supported by appropriate, distribution and promotion. Low prices may result in quicker penetration and target segment wants this and competition permits. Globally, the pricing must consider costs and then be adopted to local requirements in foreign markets but, at the same time, it must be consistent with the firms worldwide objectives, such as profit maximization, ROI (Return on Investment), or market – share, In the global arena the complexity and scope of pricing tends to raise the member of countries. The Global pricing decisions should include the fees, tariffs, special taxes, additional packaging, labeling, shipping middle – men costs, additional risks, insurance, and financing costs arising from varying levels of inflation and fluctuation in currency rates.

Pricing Objectives:

A firm's pricing objectives is one of the most important determinants of its profit. A firm's pricing policy has the following objectives.

i) Market Share:

The price may be manipulated to increase the market share. In many cases it is a corollary to market penetration.

ii) Market Penetration:

Market Penetration may be a very important objective, particularly for new exporters. A firm may attempt to penetrate the market with a low price.

iii) Fighting Competition:

Sometimes price is a tool to fight competition. A price reduction by the competitor may have to be countered by price cuts. Sometimes, price cuts may be affected to discipline the competitor or to compel the competitor to reduce prices so that his cash flows will be affected.

iv) Preventing New Entry:

A firm charges a low price even when there is scope for high price so that the industry does not look very attractive to new entrants.

v) Market Skimming:

This is used for innovative products. The product is introduced with a high initial price to skim the cream of the market; the price may be subsequently reduced to achieve greater market penetration.

vi) Early Cash Recovery:

A firm with liquidity problem might give priority to generate a better cash flow. Hence, it adopts a pricing that might help it liquidate the stock and/ or encourage prompt payment by the channel members or buyers.

vii) Optimum Capacity Utilization:

Exporting is sometimes resorted to enable the firm to achieve optimum capacity utilization so as to minimize the unit cost of production. In such a case, achieving the required of exports could be the objective of export pricing.

viii) Shorten Payback Period:

When the market is uncertain and risky because of factors like swift technological changes, short product lifecycles, political reasons, threat of potential competition, etc., recouping the investment as early as possible would be an important objective.

ix) Meeting Export Obligation:

A company with specific export obligation may be compelled to adopt a pricing policy that enables it to discharge its export obligation. Sometimes it may even imply a price lower than the cost.

x) Profit Maximization:

In many cases, the primary pricing objective is maximization of profits.

xii) Return on Investment:

Achieving the target rate of return is the most important pricing objective in a number of cases.

xiii) Disposal of Surplus:

A company confronted with a surplus stock may resort to exporting to dispose of the surplus. In such cases, exports sometimes take the form of dumping.

To establish an overseas price, we need to consider many of the same factors involved in pricing for the domestic market. These factors include competition; costs such as production, packaging, transportation and handling, promotion and selling expenses; the demand for the product or service and the maximum price that the market is willing to pay.

FACTORS INFLUENCING EXPORT PRICING DECISIONS:

For a Global Marketing Management, the influencing factors are very important. The differences in culture, the economic environment and political and legal factors are considered as important in global marketing.

I. SOCIAL AND CULTURAL FACTORS:

Culture is a set of shared value passed down from generation to generation in a society. These values determine the socially acceptable behaviour. Some of the Cultural elements are given below.

a) Family:

In some countries the family is extremely closely inter related, whereas in some other countries the family members act more independently.

b) Social customs and Behaviour:

The social customs in practice and Customary behaviour varies from one country to another.

c) Education:

The literacy level influences advertising, branding and labeling. The Brand mark may become a dominant marketing strategy. When customers look into the label they see mainly for the picture in the label.

d) Language Differences

Some words may have different meanings is some language. Therefore it is better to print the contents of label in the local and national language. If possible in the international language – English also.

II) POLITICAL AND LEGAL FACTORS.

The Stability of government and its attitudes towards free trade is more important. The major legal forces affecting global markets are the barriers created by governments to restrict trade to protect domestic industries.

The following are some of such barriers.

a) Tariff:

This is normally a tax imposed on a product, entering a country. The tariffs are used to protect the domestic producers. For example, Japan has a very high tariff on imported. rice.

b) Import Quota:

This is a limitation on the amount of a particular product that may be brought into a country. Like tariffs, the quotas are also intended to protect the local industries.

c) Local content law:

This is a regulation, specifying the particular proportion of a finished products components and labour which must be provided by the importing country. A firm may import most of the products parts and buy some parts locally and have the final product assembled locally. These laws are used, to provide jobs and protect domestic industries.

III) TRADE AGREEMENTS:

These trade agreements will reduce the trade barriers by giving preferential treatment to the firms in the member – countries. By analyzing the major trade agreements, we can form an impression of the role they play in global marketing.

a) The General Agreement on Tariffs and Trade (GATT):

This agreement was created in 1948 to develop certain fair trade practices among members. Presently, about 100 nations participate in its periodical negotiations, on such issues like tariff reductions, import restrictions, subsidization of industry by government etc,

b) The European Community (E.C):

A political and economic alliance was evolved among to countries (France, Italy, Belgium, West Germany, Luxembourg and Netherlands) under the Treaty of Rome in 1957. This was otherwise known as the European Common Market.

The aim of the E.C. is a single market for its members who would permit the free movement of goods, services, people and capital. The member – countries would be governed by the same set of rules for transporting goods, etc.

c) The European Free Trade Association (EFTA):

This association was formed in 1960, with a view to eliminate most of the trade barriers between the member countries. In 1992, a treaty was reached between EFTA and E.C. towards the single market concept.

d) The North American Free Trade Agreement (NAFTA):

The Governments of U.S.A. and Canada have entered into an Agreement in 1989, with the intention of eliminating tariffs between them for a period of 10 Years.

TYPES OF PRICING

The common methods of pricing exports are:

● *Domestic Pricing:*

Domestic Pricing is a common but not necessarily accurate method of pricing exports. This type of pricing uses the domestic price of the product or service as a base and adds export costs, including packaging, shipping and insurance. Because the domestic price already includes an allocation of domestic marketing costs, prices determined using the method might be too high to be competitive.

● *Incremental cost pricing:*

Incremental cost pricing determines a basic unit cost that takes into account the costs of producing and selling products for export, and then adds a markup to arrive at the desired profit margin. To determine a price using this method, first establish the "export base cost" by stripping profit markup and the cost of domestic selling. In addition to the base cost, include genuine export expenses (export overheads, special packing, shipping, port charges, insurance, overseas commissions, and allowance for sales promotion and advertising) and the unit price necessary to yield the desired profit margin.

● *Cost modification:*

Cost modification involves reducing the quality of an item by using cheaper materials, simplifying the product or modifying your marketing program, which lowers the price.

● *Cost plus Pricing:*

One of the most common methods of calculating export pricing is the Cost Plus Approach. This approach takes the appropriate component of your domestic price and includes any export related costs that will be incurred, depending on the agreed Incoterms.

While relatively straight forward, this approach does not consider the ultimate selling price in the export market, and how your product will be priced against competitive products. As a result, some products may not be successful in the export market as their price structure is not competitive.

Top down Pricing:

Top Down pricing turns the Cost Plus approach on its head by looking at the pricing of competitive products in the export market. By starting at looking at retail pricing, removing distributor and importer margins, duties, freight, insurance etc etc, you can determine desired price points across different Incoterms.

The Top Down approach will allow you to determine the margin levels which can be obtained in different markets. While some markets may require reduced margins to be competitive, other markets may present opportunities for higher margins. Using this approach in conjunction with your importer or distributor will enable you to set the pricing at a level in which you believe your product will have the most success.

Differential or Marginal Pricing

Differential or Marginal pricing is an approach commonly used for export. By looking at the fixed and variable costs in a business, you will ultimately determine your domestic pricing. However by factoring an allowance for increased export sales, the fixed costs are effectively reduced on a per unit basis.

Consider the following example:

DOMESTIC: 100,000 units sold per year

Fixed Costs: $200,000 per year

Variable Costs: $5 per unit

Total Costs: $700,000

Total Cost per unit: $7 per unit

DOMESTIC + EXPORT: 150,000 units sold per year

Fixed Costs: $200,000 per year

Variable Costs: $5 per unit

Total Costs: $950,000

Total Cost per unit: $6.33

Before fixing the price, it is important to determine all components which make up the final cost of goods and who is responsible to pay them. Such costs include:

- Export Customs Clearance
- Packing
- Freight

- Insurance
- l   It is important to realise that these costs may vary from country to country and customer to customer. By allowing for increased production to cater for an export market, the total costs per unit are reduced, allowing to potentially selling in an export market at a lower price level with the same level of profit.

When preparing an export price list, in many cases, a range of costs may apply, such as:

- Fixed costs such as salaries or rents, etc.
- Custom duty, customs clearance, import duty and taxes
- Sea or air freight and insurance
- Custom broker's fee, agent's commission or importer's mark-up
- Ex ship, transportation from port of entry to customer
- Break-bulk fees (if third party warehouse applies)
- Warehousing fees, packaging and labelling to local standards
- Product certification, if required and product liability insurance
- Advertising and promotional costs, etc

    Dumping occurs when firms start using price discrimination as a strategy for profit maximisation.

DUMPING:

Dumping, is a pricing practice where a firm charges a lower price for exporting goods than it does for the same goods sold domestically. It is said to be the most common form of price discrimination in international trade. Dumping can only occur at places where imperfect competition and where the markets are segmented in a way such that domestic residents cannot easily purchase goods intended for export. It is a subtle measure of protection which comes under the non-tariff barriers and is product and source specific.

Antidumping duties were initiated withthe intention of nullifying the effect of the market distortions created due to unfair trade practices adopted by aggressive exports. They are meant to be remedial and not punitive in nature. A harmful to the domestic producers as their products are unable to compete with the artificially low prices imposed by the imported goods. As a method of protection to the domestic industries, Anti dumping duties are thus levied on the exporting country which has been accused of dumping goods in another country. As the antidumping duty is only meant to provide protection to the domestic firms in the initial stages, as per the international laws, the antidumping legislations may last for a maximum period of five years.

Antidumping measures are of two kinds:

- *Antidumping duty:*

This is imposed at the time of imports, in addition to other customs duties. The purpose of antidumping duty is to raise the price of the commodity when introduced in the market of the importing country.

- *Price undertaking:*

If the exporter himself undertakes to raise the price of the product then the importing country can consider it and accept it instead of imposing antidumping duty.

The conditions mandatory for dumping to take place are:

- Presence of an imperfect market where price discrimination between markets is possible.(Because in imperfect market firms are price setters not price takers).

- Segmented markets where there is no arbitrage easily possible between markets.

Only if the above two conditions are satisfied is it profitable for the exporting firm to engage in dumping.

Types of Dumping:

Dumping can be of three types. They are:

1) Sporadic Dumping:

Sporadic Dumping refers to setting the excess stock which arises occasionally. The main aim of the firms is to liquidate the excess stock and do not have great interest in getting a market position.

2) Intermittent Dumping:

Intermittent Dumping refers to the sale of goods in a foreign market at a price lower than the home market. The main aim of these firms is to capture and retain a market position rather than liquidation of stocks. Additionally, this enables the firm to combat and eliminate competitors.

3) Long-period Dumping:

Long-period Dumping refers to facilitate the utilization of full capacity of the plant continuously. This leads to lowering of costs and improvement of profits in the home market.

2.7   INSPECTION AND QUALITY CONTROL

Concept of Quality:

Quality of a product is defined a set of attributes or specifications including packaging specifications in relation to a given product it is the manufacturer who first decides the quality of a product before introducing it in the market. Quality is maintained by keeping in view the national or the international standards of quality as and down by the respective rational or international standards bodies. The level of quality – high medium or low-depends upon how rich or poor these specifications are, If the specifications are of very high order the level of quality would be high and if the specifications are poor or weak, then the quality would be termed as low quality.

Between the high and low quality lies the medium range of the quality. These quality specifications may then be modified during negotiations with the foreign buyer to suit their requirements. Finally, the quality of the export product is determined with reference to the specifications as laid down by the buyer.

Objectives of quality control on pre-shipment of goods:

The following are some of the objectives of quality control for exports.

1.   Promotion and ensuring the image of Indian goods exported to other countries.

2.   Ensuring goods of assured quality only move in to the export markets

3.   Sustaining the foreign markets where Indian goods are already favoured and developing new markets with competitive quality.

4.   Ensuring sound and safe performance of the products without causing any health or safety hazards.

5. Maintaining proper packaging for the safety of the product during transit.

6. Elimination the causes of complaints from the foreign buyers and making every effort to spread quality consciousness in the country to improve overall quality of Indian products.

NEED FOR PRE-SHIPMENT INSPECTIONS:

An exporter would face competition from both inland and foreign countries. Hence formulation of appropriate strategies is important. The goods should be properly inspected to ensure that the quality of the export goods is maintained as desired by the buyer. Goods of poor quality spoil not only their own market buy also bring bad name to the image of the country itself. It is, thus, in the business interest of the exporter to send shipment of the right quality to the buyer. This would also facilitate effective penetration and sustenance in the export markets by improving the brand image of the goods. The Government of India had also recognized the need for effective pre-shipment inspection long back in 1963 itself when the Export (Quality Control and inspection) Act, 1963 was enacted to provide for sound development of the export trade through quality control and pre-shipment inspection.

Types of pre-shipment inspection:

There are primarily two different types of pre-shipment inspection namely:

i)   Voluntary Inspection

ii) Compulsory Inspection

i) Voluntary Inspection:

The following are the different forms of voluntary pre-shipment inspection of the export shipments.

1) By the exporter himself

2) By the buyer's representative

3) By the buying agent in the exporter's country

4) By the inspection agencies in the private sector

ii) Compulsory Inspection:

Compulsory Pre-shipment inspection is conducted by the following agencies of the Government of India.

1)   Export Inspection Council through as Export Inspection Agencies

2)   Textile Committee

3)   Development Commissioner (Handicrafts)

4)   Central Silk Board

Export Inspection Council of India.

Exported goods represent a country's image, in terms of its commitment to quality and perfection. If you import goods from a supplier from a particular country and they turn out to be defective or do not measure up to your expectations, you will not only form a poor impression about the exporter but also about the country under question. Exporters, no doubt, work hard to ensure that goods conform to expected standards. However, since exports reflect a nation's quality as well, the Government of India has also taken upon itself the onus of making sure that exports from India conform to international quality norms. To accomplish this task, the Export (Quality Control and Inspection) Act, 1963 was established and later amended in 1984. The basic objective of the Act is to ensure sound development of export trade of India through Quality Control and Inspections.

The Export Inspection Council (EIC) was set up by the Government of India under Section 3 of the Export (Quality Control and Inspection) Act, 1963 (22 of 1963), as an advisory body to the Central Government, which is empowered to:

- Notify commodities which will be subject to quality control and/or inspection prior to export

- Establish standards of quality for notified commodities

- Specify the type of quality control and/or inspection to be applied to such commodities.

EIC has evolved a great deal and stands as an apex institution having the vision to facilitate worldwide access for Indian exports through a credible and efficient inspection and certification system which can help an earn global recognition as India's premier organization for certifying quality.

Functions:

- Certification of quality of export commodities through installation of quality assurance systems (in-process quality control and self-certification) in exporting units as well as consignment-wise inspection.

- Certification of quality of food items for export through installation of Food Safety Management Systems in the food processing units as per international standards.

- Issue of different types of certificates such as health, authenticity etc. to exporters under various product schemes for export.

- Issue of Certificates of Origin to exporters under various preferential tariff schemes for export products.

- Laboratory testing services.

- Training and technical assistance to the industry in installation of Quality and Safety Management Systems based on principles of Hazard Analysis Critical Control Point (HACCP), ISO-9001:2000, ISO: 17025 and other related international standards, laboratory testing etc.

- Recognition of Inspection Agencies as per ISO: 17020 and Laboratories as per ISO: 17025 and utilizing them for export inspection and testing.

- In rendering the above services, EIAs are backed by qualified technical manpower, having nearly 40 years of diversified experience of quality control and inspection of notified commodities including their testing as per international standards/importing countries' standards or the foreign buyer's specifications.

EIC advises the Central Government on measures to be taken for development of export trade through quality control and pre-shipment inspection. EIAs are the five Export Inspection Agencies which have headquarters at Mumbai, Kolkata, Cochin, Delhi and Chennai. EIAs are the autonomous field organizations for implementing policies of the Central Government with respect to quality control and/or pre-shipment inspection of export commodities from India.

Notification of Commodities:

Notification commodities represent products that are subject to compulsory pre-shipment inspection under Section 6 of the Export (Quality Control & Inspection) Act 1963. There are over 1,200 Commodities under the broad classifications of chemicals and allied products, cement concrete, common salt, inorganic pigments, linoleum, minerals and ores group, organic chemicals, paint and allied products, pesticides and their formulations, printing ink, PVC leather, cloth refractories, rubber products, cycle tyres and tubes, bicycle and rickshaw tubes, bicycle and rickshaw tyres, rubber belts, v.belts, fan belts, rubber hoses, engineering products, automobile – spares components and accessories, bicycles bright steel bars, cast iron manholes covers and frames, cast iron soil pipes and fittings, cast iron spun pipes, diesel engines, dry-batteries, electric cables and conductors, electric fans, electric lamps and tubes, electric motors and generators, enamelware, fasteners, gas cylinders, household electrical appliances, jute mill spares, accessories, light engineering products, builders hardwares. Cutlery, household articles, pipe fitting, stainless steel utensil. Steel and steel product, storage batteries, switch gear and control gear, food and agricultural products, fish and fishery products. Canned crab meat prawns (frozen), dried fish, egg products, fruits and vegetable products, textiles, coir products, coir yarn (baled), hand knotted woolen carpets, jute and jute products, footwear and footwear components, human hair double drawn, at present that fall under the purview of these notifications.

Export Certification Systems:

The following Export Certification System is available with EIC:

Consignment-wise Inspection – Under this system, each export consignment is inspected and tested by the recognized inspection agency. Samples are drawn using statistical methods and the shipment is tested against prescribed standards. These tests may be carried out either in the field or at any recognized laboratory, depending upon the requirements. If the goods pass the test, a certificate to that effect is issued that enables the exporter to gain clearance at customs. However, if the goods are not found conforming to standards, the shipment is rejected. The exporter will have to re-apply for inspection after he has carried out necessary improvements.

These certificates usually have a validity period and if the exporter is unable to ship the goods within such this period. He will have to-apply and obtain a fresh certificate.

No consignment of any notified commodity can be exported unless it is accompanied by a certificate issued by a recognised inspection agency. Customs authorities will not grant their approval, unless this certificate is produced.

Chapter-III

3.1 CUSTOM CLEARANCE OF EXPORT AND IMPORT CARGO

Customs Clearance Formalities:

According the Section 40 of, the Customs Act, the person in-charge of the conveyance vessel, Vehicle, in craft, etc., cannot permit loading of export cargo at the Customs Station unless and until format permission to the export given by the authorized Customs Officer is presented.

Before granting the permission, the Customs Officer ensures that the goods being exported are in accordance with different regulations, particularly in terms of the following:

a)   The goods are of the same type, sort and value as have been declared by the exporter.

b)   The duty or success leviable thereon has been properly determined and paid

c)   Provisions of Export (Control) Order, Export (Quality/ Control and Inspection) Act and Foreign Exchange (Regulation) Act are complied with.

Legal Frame work:

Section 50 of the Indian Customs Act requires the exporter to file a declaration in a prescribed form and submit supporting documents to enable the customs authorities to cheek declarations made by the exporter.

The objectives of the customs control are:

i)   To ensure that nothing goes out of the country against the laws of the land and that prohibitions and restrictions regarding outward cargo are duly enforced by the customs-authorities.

ii)   To ensure authenticity of the value of outward cargo according to the customs Valuation rules to check over and under invoicing.

iii) To assess and realize export duty/charge according to the customs Tariff Act and any other fiscal legislations;

iv) To check that all the relevant regulatory provisions enforced by various authorities in the country have been duly complied with in respect of export and

v) To provide export data through the customs returns.

Customs clearance stages:

There are four stages of customs involvement. There are:

1) Processing of documents at the Customs House i.e., the main officer. This stage involves:

    i) Checking up of documents to ensure that all relevant documents have been submitted,

    ii) Verification of quantity and value of goods,

    iii) Verification and determination of rate of duty and collection of the duty amount,

    iv) Direction for the customs officer in the docks for physical examination of goods;

2) Physical examination of goods in the docks in accordance with the examination' order given at the Customs House;

3) Supervision of loading by the customs Preventive Officer and

4) Post-shipment endorsement by the Customs Preventive Officer.

DOCUMENTARY REQUIREMENTS

For movement of goods by air or by sea, the customs permission for shipment is given on a prescribed document, known as Shipping Bill. In other cases (Le.by road/rail) the document is known as Bill of Export. There are four types of Shipping Bill/Bill of export,

1. Dutiable Shipping Bill/Bill of Export for those goods which attract export duty/cess:

2. Drawback Shipping Bill/Bill of Export for those goods which are covered by the Duty drawback Scheme,

3. Free Shipping Bill/Bill of Export for those goods which are neither attract export duty/cess nor are covered by the Duty Drawback scheme,

4. Ex-bond Shipping Bill/Bill of Export for those goods which are shipped from, the customs, bonded warehouse.

The Exporter or his agent submits the following documents to the customs department

- Shipping Bill (in duplicate, triplicate or quadruplicate) duly filled in and signed.
- Declaration regarding truth of statement made in the Shipping Bill
- Invoice copy
- R Form
- Export License (wherever required)
- Quality Control Inspection Certificate (wherever required)
- Original Contract wherever available or correspondence leading to contract
- Contract registration certificate (wherever applicable)
- Letter of credit (wherever applicable)
- Packing List
- AR4/ARS Forms (original and duplicate)
- Any other documents

3.2 THE SHIPPING AND CUSTOMS FORMALITIES AND THE PROCEDURE FOR SHIPPING AND CUSTOMS CLEARANCE

The following is the procedure for shipping and customs clearance

i) Preparation and Submission of Export Documents:-

For the clearance of cargo from customs, the exporter his agent has to submit the following set of documents along with five copies of shipping bill to the Customs Appraiser at the Custom House.

- Letter of Credit along with the export contract or export order,
- Commercial Invoice (2 copies),
- Packing List of Packing Note,
- Certificate of Origin,
- GR Form (original and duplicate),

- ARE-I Form,
- Original copy of Certificate of Inspection, where necessary,
- Marine Insurance Policy.

ii) Verification of Documents:-

The Customs appraiser verifies the details listed in each document and ensures that all the formalities relating to exchange control, quality control. If Pre-shipment inspection and licensing have been compiled with by the exporter, The customs appraise issues a Shipping Bill Number.

iii) Valuation of the Goods:-

The Customs Appraiser assesses the shipping bill and values the goods. The value of goods as determined by the Customs. Appraiser is considered for all future transactions, especially for the claim of incentives. All documents are returned to the exporter or his agent except:

- Original copy of GR to be forwarded to the RBI
- Original copy of Shipping Bill
- One copy of Commercial Invoice:

The Validity of assessed shipping bill is for one month only. If the exporter fails to deliver the goods in that period; he will have to undergo the above procedure again.

iv) Obtaining 'Carting Order' from the Port Trust Authorities:

The C&F agent, then, approaches the Superintendent of the concerned Port Trust for obtaining the 'Carting Order' for moving the cargo inside the dock. After obtaining the Carting Order, the cargo is physically moved into the port area and stored in the appropriate shed.

v) Customs Examination and Issue of Let Export Order:

The Customs Examiner at the port of shipment physically examines the goods and seals the packages in his presence. The same can be arranged for at the factory or warehouse of the exporter by making an application to the Assistant Collector of Customs. The Customs Examiner, if satisfied, issues a formal permission for the loading of cargo on the ship in the form of a 'Let Export Order' The above procedure is now processed through Electronic Data Interchange (EDI) System.

vi) Obtaining 'Let Ship Order' from the Customs Preventive Officer:-

'Let Export Order' must be supplemented by a 'Let Ship Order' issued by the Customs   Preventive Officer. The C&F agency submits the duplicate copy of Shipping Bill, duly endorsed by the Customs Examiner, to the Customs Preventive Officer who endorses it with the 'Let Ship Order'.

vii) Obtaining Mate's Receipt and Bill of Lading:-

The goods are then loaded on board the ship for which the Mate or the Captain of the ship issues Mate's Receipt to the Port Superintendent. The Port Superintendent, on receipt of port dues. Hands over the Mate's Receipt to the C&F Agent. The II C&F Agent surrenders the Mate's Receipt to the Shipping Company for obtaining the Bill of loading. The Shipping Company issues two to three negotiable and two to three non-negotiable copies of Bill of Lading.

3.3   THE PROCEDURE FOR REALISATION OF EXPORT PROCEEDS

The following is the procedure for the realization of export proceeds.

a) Presentation of Documents to the Bank for Negotiation:

After shipment of goods the expectation required to submit the shipping documents to an authorized dealer within 21 days of the date for negotiation. Submission of relevant documents to the bank and the process of getting the payment train the bank are called "Negotiation of the Documents" and the documents are called Negotiable Set of Documents'. The Set normally contains:

- Bill of Exchange, Sight Draft or Usance Draft
- Full set of Bill of Lading or Airway Bill
- Original Letter of Credit
- Customs Invoice
- Commercial Invoice including one copy duly certified by the Customs.
- Packing List.
- Foreign exchange declaration form.   GR/SOFTEX/PP forms in duplicate.
- Exchange control copy of the Shipping Bill.

- Certificate of Origin, GSP or APR Certificate, etc.
- Marine Insurance Policy, in duplicate.

b) Dispatch of Documents:

The bank negotiates these documents to the importer's bank in the manner as specified in the L/C. Before negotiating documents, the exporter's bank scrutinises them in order to ensure that all formalities have been complied with and all documents are in order. The bank then sends the Bank Certificate and attested copies of commercial invoice to the exporter.

- **Acceptance of the bill of exchange:** Bill of exchange accompanied by the above documents is known as dle Documentary Bill of Exchange. It is of two types:-

- **Documents against Payment (Sight Drafts):-** In case of sight draft, the drawer instructs the bank to hank over relevant documents to the importer only against payment.

- **Documents against acceptance (Usance Draft):-** (P case of usance draft, the drawer instructs the bank to hand over the relevant documents to the importer against his 'acceptance' of the bill of exchange.

- **Letter of Indemnify:-** The exporter can get immediate payment from his bank on the submission of documents by signing a letter of indemnity. By signing the letter of indemnity the exporter undertakes to indemnify the bank in the event of non-receipt of payment from the importer along with accrued interests.

- **Realization of Export Proceeds:** On receiving the documentary bill of exchange, the importer releases payment in case of sight draft or accepts the usance draft undertaking to pay on maturity of the bill of exchange. The exporter's bank receives the payment through importer's bank and is credited to exporter's account.

- **Processing of GR form:** On receiving the export proceeds the exporter's bank intimates the same to the RBI by recording the fact on the duplicate copy of GR. The RBI verifies the details in duplicate copy of GR with the original copy of GR received from the Customs. If the details are found to be in order then the export transaction is treated to be completed.

3.4   METHODS OF PAYMENT AVAILABLE FOR EXPORT:

- Advance Payment
- Open Account
- Consignment Sales
- Documents against Acceptance (D/A)
- Documents against Payment (D/P)
- Letter of Credit (LC)

Advance Payment

It is the safest payment option where the importer sends the payment in advance to the exporter either through TT (Telegraphic Transfer) or through a cheque or demand draft. This is normally done after acceptance of the order by the exporter. The exporter is safe as he will ship the goods only at a later date, He also gets a ready solution to his liquidity problem as he can use the funds towards production of the export order. He needs to deposit the cheque/demand draft with his bank and obtain an FIRC (Foreign Inward Remittance Certificate).

This method, however, is not safe for the buyer and therefore is not preferred. However, is cases of very small amounts or where there is extreme trust, this method may be used. For example, for an order amount of US$250/500 or even 1000,, this seems to be the only appropriate mode. Another situation could be of a son exporting from India, to his father in the U.K. Here there is apparently no risk, so advance payment can be used. This method is also used by foreign affiliates of exporters. This method is the least expensive as no interest/commission is required to be paid anywhere and it is also the least complicated, as it does not involve any procedural formalities/documentation.

Open Account:

This is an arrangement between the buyer and the exporter where goods are shipped without the guarantee of payments. Both the parties agree on sales terms but no documentary evidence is created. The accounts between the exporter and buyer are settled periodically. Since the chances of default or delay in payment are very high under this system, the exporter must deal with only trustworthy buyers.

This system suits the importer as he obtains delivery of the goods without having to pay for them. As the importer need not arrange any finances, there is saving on expenses, time and effort.

The exporter has to have financial resources to carry out the export order without any payment. He needs to safeguard his interests by checking the track record of the buyer thoroughly before agreeing to such an arrangement. Consignment Sales:

Under this method, goods are shipped by the exporter but he transfers the ownership to the importer only when the goods are actually sold. This means that the entire risk is borne by the exporter. If the Importer is unable to find an actual buyer, the exporter is jumped with the unsold goods and he can not claim payment for the same from the importer.

The exporter's funds are blocked throughout this period and he is responsible for additional expenses such as interest, warehousing costs, commissions, insurance charge etc. This arrangement is full of uncertainties as the exporter is not exporter is not sure of the actual sale, timeframe and the price realization. However, his responsibility for payment realization remains absolute as he has to declare the expected value of the shipment on the GR form.

Consignment exports offer a chance of earning higher prices in markets abroad. Exporter who has their own branches/affiliates in the foreign countries with control over sales would best suit for this system. He should also be financially sound to manage longer periods of uncertainty and bear additional expenses.

Usually in the trade of agro exports (accept onion, rice and other cereals, mango pulp), the importer never provides a Letter of Credit (L/C). Such export is done on a consignment basis, and payment as per actual sales is made.

Under the D/A method, the exporter sends the shipment documents along with the draft (bill of exchange) through his bank to the importer's bank that gets the draft accepted by the importer before handing him over the title documents. The importer thus gets the title to the shipment against his acceptance of the bill of exchange for the value of the shipment. These drafts are normally readied for presentation after 30/45/60/90 days from the date of acceptance. The exporter presents the same on the due date to the buyer's bank through his bank, and gets his payment. The system provides for delivery of ownership documents against acceptance of an instrument of debt.

There is a great risk for the exporter, as the bill may not be honoured by the buyer on presentation. The buyer certainly is safe as he gets the delivery of the shipment much before the due date for payment. The exporter will have to face a lot of difficulty and losses, in case the buyer does not honour his commitment.

Documents against Payment (D/P)

The documents are sent to the buyer's bank with a draft (bill of exchange). However, this draft is a sight draft and not a usance draft. This draft has to be paid immediately on sight and only after the receipt of payment the shipment title documents are released, is the importer gets possession of the ownership documents of the shipment only after making payment for the same. The exporter, on the other hand, release possession of shipment title papers only against the receipt of payment. No credit is involved here.

This system is definitely safer than the D/A method, as sight drafts allow for release of goods only against payments.

Letter of Credit (LC)

A letter of credit is a very popular form of documentary credit. In fact, majority of international business transactions use LCs. The letter of credit is a letter established by the importer through his bank to the benefit of the exporter promising payment of drafts drawn against this letter if the exporter complies with the specific conditions prescribed in the LC. The conditions are usually the same as stipulated in the purchase order or export contract. Lc acts as a substitution of the importer's promise to that of his bank's to the exporter to honour its commitment to pay for the export bills provided all conditions are satisfied. In this way, a letter of credit works as an independent contract between the exporter (designated beneficiary) and the issuing bank.

More formally, a letter of credit can be defined as " A binding document that a buyer can request from his bank in order to guarantee that the payment for goods will be transferred to the seller. Basically, a letter of credit provides reassurance to the seller that he will receive the payment for the goods. In order for the payment to occur, the seller has to present the bank with the necessary shipping documents confirming the delivery of goods within a given time frame. It is often used in international trade to eliminate risks such as unfamiliarity with the foreign country, customs, or political instability

All LCs should be drawn as per the guidelines of UCP 500 (Uniform Customs and Practices for Documentary Credits) of the International Chambers of Commerce (ICC). These were last revised in 1993 and the latest revision is currently under progress.

Benefits of LCs

Letters of Credit offer certain advantages to both the exporter and the importer. These are explained below:

To Exporters:

- LC minimizes the credit risk provided the issuing bank is reputed and carries a sound track record.
- LC eliminates risk of payment delays due to uncertain factors like political instability.
- LC affords financing for the exporter. All nationalized banks in India are more than willing to finance an exporter who has an export order backed by an LC from a reputed foreign bank.
- LC normally will have a stabilizing effect on production by the exporter as the exporter is bound to ship by a certain date as per the LC, failing which the order will stand cancelled.
- LC minimizes uncertainty and provides a clear picture to the exporter regarding all the requirements for payments.

To Importers:

- The importer placing orders on exporters backed by LCs commands a great respect and bargaining power. He is in a position to ask for better prices and faster deliveries.
- Use of LCs will attract a large number of good suppliers offering the importer a lot of choice.
- The importer is assured of timely shipment of the specified quality and quantity of ordered merchandise. Documents under LC like on-board Bill of Lading (B/L) and Inspections Certificate by a buyer nominated agency will serve this purpose well.
- The importer can refuse payment if he finds any and even a very minor mistake/ oversight (referred to as a Document Discrepancy) in any of the required documents. This affords him a very tight

control over the exporter. Ensuring accuracy of shipment and related paperwork.

• Importer's risk of losing money in case the supplier is unable or unwilling to effect a proper shipment is totally eliminated.

Types of LCs

There are several types of LCs. It is important for an exporter to know all the types so that while finalizing an export deal, he will be in a better position to ask for the right kind of LC from the importer.

Documentary and Clean LCs: A documentary LC is the one that requires the exporter to submit certain documents like commercial invoice, packing list, customs invoice, inspection certificate, certificate of origin, etc. together with the draft to the issuing bank. Most of the LCs used in export / import fall under this category. A clean LC, is one that does not require presentation of any documents. Clean LCs are normally used for escrow arrangements and bank guarantees.

Revocable and Irrevocable LCs: An LC is revocable when it is used only as a means of arranging payment and carries no guarantee. It can be withdrawn without any notice at any time upto the time of presentation of drafts under LC for payment to the issuing bank. An irrevocable LC, to the contrary, carries both a payment arrangement and guarantee of payment and therefore, cannot be revoked without the consent of all parties involved including the exporter. Most international transactions use irrevocable LCs.

Confirmed and Unconfirmed LCs: A letter of credit may be confirmed or unconfirmed. A confirmed letter of credit creates obligations on both the issuing as well as confirming bank to honour the commitment under the LC. It works as a double protection for the beneficiary. An unconfirmed LC creates this obligation only on the issuing bank.

The confirming bank could either be a local bank in the country of the exporter or a foreign bank, depending on the arrangements that the issuing bank has. The issuing bank issues the LC and another bank confirms it. Thus, both these banks undertake to comply with the provisions of the LC. Exporters, therefore, generally prefer an irrevocable confirmed LC issued by a prime bank.

Special LCs:

There are certain types of LCs that fall under this Category. The most popular ones are:

- Revolving LCs are those where the maturity period or the amount prescribed automatically gets renewed subject to the mutually agreed terms and conditions at the time of setting up of the LC under the export contract.

Revolving LCs can be of two types - Cumulative and Non-cumulative.

Cumulative revolving LCs will automatically apply/add the the unutilized amount during a given time and the same will be carried over to the next period.

Non-cumulative LCs will consider the unutilized amount in a given time as lapsed and will not add this to be carried over to the next period.

- Transferable LCs are those under which the beneficiary is given the right to transfer the benefits available under the LC to one or more secondary beneficiaries. No LC can be transferred unless it specifically authorizes to do so. The LC itself has to contain a transferability clause.

This has functional advantages. The exporter can use the LC transfer to enable his suppliers to raise working capital on the strength of the LC. This saves him the entire process of arranging finance to pay his suppliers to buy goods from them. This is also very practical and convenient. The suppliers also can make use of the creditworthiness of the original buyer.

- Back-to-Back LCs is those where exporters are able to use the original LC as a cover to open another LC in favour of their local suppliers. The original LC serves as a security to the bank issuing the back-to-back LC in favour of the exporter's suppliers. The arrangement is quite convenient as the exporter is able to use his buyer's credit to finance his suppliers' operations. However, the back-to-back LC issuing bank assumes double risk that of the exporter's as well as of the primary banks. Due to this reason, many banks are not too keen on issuing back-to-back LCs.

Chapter –IV

4.1 EXPORT ORDER

Introduction:

- Export order must confirm to the terms of contract and then sent to the overseas buyer.

- But before its confirmation, it must be scrutinized with regards to products and their specifications, terms of payment, price,, delivery schedule etc.,

- The immediate task of exporter is to acknowledge the export order which is different from its acceptance.

  Parameter required for export order

1) Nature:

Export order is a document, or communication the decision of foreign buyer to purchase items from exporter. It would clearly indicate the exporter's pro-forma invoice / quotation number and its date, including item quantity price delivery date, shipping marks, insurance. Payment terms, documents required etc. Before acceptance, the export order should be scrutinized in all aspects.

2) Acknowledgement:

The exporter should write a simple letter to overseas buyer thanking him for the export order and stating that the confirmation of the same would be sent soon.

3) Scrutiny:

The export order should be carefully scrutinized in terms of pro forma invoice/contract sent to the foreign buyer, on the following aspects:

- The order has been received for same products for which quotation/offer was sent.

- Size and specifications are also as per quotation/offer. Unit measurement needs to be specified as well. It could be numbers, volume, or weight.

- Ordered quantity both in words and figures. This is essential to leave out any room for confusion. Pre-shipment inspection is as per agreed in pro-forma invoice. Pre-shipment inspection can be done by the following persons:

- Exporter

- Inspection by exporter nominated agency

- Inspection by importer nominated agency

- Export Inspection Agency (EIA) GO authorized agency.

1) Confirmation:

If the exporter is satisfied on various aspects mentioned in the export order he should send a formal confirmation to the overseas buyer.

2) Clarification:

If the exporter is not completely satisfied with the terms of export order, clarification should be ought from the buyer before its confirmation.

The clarification could be in terms of:

- Quantity

- Delivery schedule

- Terms of payment

- INCO terms etc.

The delivery period should be specific and not in terms like "immediate delivery", or "as soon as possible."

4.2 CONTENTS OF AN EXPORT ORDER / CONTRACT

An export order/contract normally covers the following:

- The item

- The description of the item

- The quantity required

- The price per unit

- The terms of payment and delivery

- Date of order/Reference to exporter's Proforma Invoice or quotation
- Date of delivery
- The kind of packaging required.
- The kind of labeling required
- The kind of marking required
- Insurance Instruction, if required
- Inspection Instruction, if required
- Documentation required
- Production sample instructions, if required
- Penalties for late delivery, if any
- Any other special conditions.

The exporter has to understand the order correctly and completely. Any misunderstanding of the order would create serious problems. In exporter must before accept the export order has to scrutinize the order thoroughly. Now a days most exports covered by Letter of credit. This is a common method of payment in the exports and it contains all the terms and conditions. Any fault or misunderstanding should be classified immediately by the exporter.

Essentials of an export contract:

1) Product:

Ordered   product's name, technical name and description, quality specifications and grades, details as to standards, sizes, references to samples and their specifications.

2) Quantity:

Ordered quantity both in figure and words, as the unit of measurement like numbers, volume or weight, should be mentioned. In addition, care has to be taken while stating the unit of measurement in international or country specific terms, for example, Metric Ton is 1,000 kgs. Whereas the US Short Ton is 907 kgs. And the British Long Ton is 1,016kgs.

3) Value:

The Total value of the order needs to be clearly stated both in numbers and words in the decided currency.

4) Packing, Labelling, and Marking Requirements:

The order must provide total details of the kind of packaging required including the labels and the marks to be put up. The instructions have to be explicit specifying requirements in full details as there could be separate labels for the articles and the packaging.

5) Mode of Payment:

This must be settled and clearly included in the contract.

6) Terms of Delivery:

The decided terms of delivery must be explicitly spelt out.

7) Consignee Details:

If the consignee is different from the buyer, his complete name and address is required.

8) Inspection Clause:

If the buyer wants a pre-shipment inspection carried out, it must be mentioned in the contract. The details of the inspection agency must also be given.

9) Production Sample:

If the buyer wants the exporter to provide him with production samples, the fact must be provided in the export order.

10) Test Certificates:

At time, the importer may ask the exporter to conduct certain tests on the material, for example, a colour bleed test or fabric, and to submit a test report by a prescribed agency. This must form a part of the contract.

11) Treatment of Various Charges:

To avoid any confusion and penalties, it must be settled and clearly instructed in the export order as to who will bear what charges / duties / taxes etc. in relation to the contract. Some of these are to be borne by the importer and some by the exporter. The export contract must specify both.

12) Period Allowed for Shipment:

The export order must clearly specify the delivery period and the due date for shipment.

13) Penalties for Delay:

The contract must also contain the possible consequences of delay in shipment by the exporter beyond the due date.

14) Insurance:

The contract must clearly provide insurance instructions for the exporter, if he wishes to arrange for insurance. Incase, the buyer is responsible for insurance, the order must say so.

15) Instructions regarding Part-shipment / Transshipment /

> *Consolidation:*
> The export contract must explicitly indicate the applicability or otherwise of any or all of these.

16) Commissions/Discounts:

In case the exporter is required to pay any kind of commission or offer any discount to the buyer or his authorized agent, the export order must provide details of the same.

17) Documents Required:

The export contract must specify all the documents required to be submitted by the exporter to the importer. The exporter then has to comply with all the documentation requirements very carefully.

18) 'Force Majeure' Clause:

Force Majeure literally means "greater force". These clauses excuse a party from liability if some unforeseen event beyond the control of that party prevents it from performing its obligations under the contract. Typically, force majeure clauses cover natural disasters or other "Acts of God", war etc. It is important to remember that force majeure clauses are intended to excuse are intended to excuse a party only if the failure to perform could not be avoided by the exercise of due care by that party. When negotiating force majeure clauses, the exporter must make sure that the clause applies equally to him as well as the importer.

19) Arbitration Clause:

The exporter must make sure that the export contract contains an arbitration clause for quick and amicable settlement of any dispute.

4.3   INCOTERMS 2000

ICC (International Chamber of Commerce) introduced the first version of Incoterms – short for "International Commercial Terms:-in 1936. Since then, ICC expert lawyers and trade practitioners have updated those six times to keep pace with the development of international trade.

Incoterms make international trade easier and help traders in different countries to understand one another. These standard trade definitions that are most commonly used in international contracts are protected by ICC copyright

Incoterms are standard trade definitions most commonly used in international sales contracts. Devised and published by the International Chamber of Commerce, they are at the heart of world trade.

Correct use of Incoterms goes a long way to providing the legal certainty upon which mutual confidence between business partners must be based.

The purpose of Incoterms is to provide a set of international rules for the interpretation of most commonly used trade terms in foreign trade. Thus, the uncertainties of different interpretations of such terms in different countries can be avoided or at least reduced to a considerable degree. The scope of Incoterms is limited to matters relating to the rights and obligations of the parties to the contract of sale with respect to the delivery of goods. Incoterms deal with a number of identified obligations imposed on the parties and the distribution of risk between the parties. In total, 13 Incoterms have been defined which are grouped into four basically different categories, applicable for sea and inland waterway transport or for all modes of transport.

	Applicable for sea transport only	Applicable for all modes of transport (including water)
Departure term		EXW (Ex Works)
Shipment term, main carriage unpaid	FAS (Free Alongside Ship) FOB (Free On Board)	FCA (Free Carrier)
Shipment term, main carriage paid	CFR (Cost and Freight) CIF (Cost, Insurance and Freight)	CPT (Carriage Paid To) CIP (Carriage and Insurance Paid to
Delivery term	DES (Delivered Ex-Ship) DEQ(Delivered Ex Quay)	DAF (Delivered At Frontier) DDU (Delivered Duty Unpaid) DDP(Delivered Duty paid)

From top (EXW) to bottom (DDP), the point of transfer in the transport chain moves from the seller's premises to the buyer's place. The second and third group specify the shipment conditions, with freight and insurance unpaid or paid. For the first three groups the risk of loss or damage during (sea) transportation are with the buyer of the goods, whereas for the fourth group, all risks up to delivery are with the seller of the goods.

An explanation of each of these with their implications is given below:

EXW EX Works (.....named place)

- Carriage to be arranged by the buyer.
- Risk transfer from the seller to the buyer when the goods are at disposal of the buyer.
- Cost transfer from the seller to the buyer when the goods are at disposal of the buyer.

FCA Free Carrier (....named place)

- Carriage to be arranged by the buyer or by the seller on the buyer's behalf.

- Risk transfer from the seller to the buyer when the goods have been delivered to the carrier at the named place.

- Cost transfer from the seller to the buyer when the goods have been delivered to the carried at the named place.

FAS Free alongside Ship (...named post of shipment)

- Carriage to be arranged by the buyer.

- Risk transfer from the seller to the buyer when the goods have been placed alongside the snip.

- Cost transfer from the seller to the buyer when the goods have been placed alongside the ship.

FOB Free On (...named port of destination)

- Carriage to be arranged by the buyer.

- Risk transfer from the seller to the buyer when the goods pass the ship's rail.

- Cost transfer from the seller to the buyer when the goods pass the ship's rail.

CFR Cost and Freight (...named port of destination)

- Carriage to be arranged by the seller

- Risk transfer from the seller to the buyer when the goods pass the ship's rail.

- Cost transfer at port of destination, buyer paying such costs as are not for the seller's account under the contract of carriage.

CIF Cost, Insurance and Freight (...named port of destination)

- Carriage and insurance to be arranged by the seller.

- Risk transfer from the seller to the buyer when the goods pass the ship's rail.

- Cost transfer at port of destination, buyer paying such costs as are not for the seller's account under the contract of carriage.

CPT Carriage paid to (duty paid) (...named place of destination)

- Carriage to be arranged by the seller.

- Risk transfer from the seller to the buyer when the goods have been delivered to the carrier.

- Cost transfer at place of destination, buyer paying such costs as are not for the seller's account under the contract carriage.

CIP Carriage and Insurance Paid to (.....named place of destination)

- Carriage and insurance to be arranged by the seller.

- Risk transfer from the seller to be buyer when the goods have been delivered to the carrier.

- Cost transfer at place of destination, buyer paying such costs as are not for the seller's account under the contract of carriage.

DAF Delivered At Frontier (....named place)

- Carriage to be arranged by the seller.

- Risk transfer from the seller to the buyer when the goods have been delivered at the frontier.

- Cost transfer from the seller to the buyer when the goods have been delivered at the frontier.

DES Delivered Ex Ship (...named port destination)

- Carriage to be arranged by the seller.

- Risk transfer from the seller to the buyer when the goods are placed at the disposal of the buyer on board the ship.

- Cost transfer from the seller to the buyer when the goods are placed at the disposal of the buyer on board the ship.

DEQ Delivered Ex Quay (...named port destination)

- Carriage to be arranged by the seller.

- Risk transfer from the seller to the buyer when the goods are placed at the disposal of the buyer on the quay.

- Cost transfer from the seller to the buyer when the goods are placed at the disposal of the buyer on the quay.

DDY Delivered Duty Unpaid (...named port destination)

- Carriage to be arranged by the seller.

- Risk transfer from the seller to the buyer when the goods are placed at the disposal of the buyer.
- Cost transfer from the seller to the buyer when the goods are placed at the disposal of the buyer.

DDP Delivered Duty Paid (...named port destination)

- Carriage to be arranged by the seller.
- Risk transfer from the seller to the buyer when the goods are placed at the disposal of the buyer.
- Cost transfer from the seller to the buyer when the goods are placed at the disposal of the buyer.

4.4 PROCESSING AN EXPORT ORDER:

Export orders must conform to the terms of contract which is sent to the foreign buyer. Before its confirmation, it must be scrutinized with regard to the products and their specifications, terms of payment, price, delivery schedule, etc.

The exporter should acknowledge the export order first and then examine the export order carefully with respect to the item, specification, preshipment inspection, payment conditions, special packaging, labeling and marking requirements, shipment and delivery date, marine insurance, documentation, etc., If the exporter is he sends a formal confirmation of the export order to the buyer. The various aspects relating to processing of an export order are discussed as under:

- *Nature:*

Export order is a document, communicating the decision of foreign buyer to purchase items from the exporter. It clearly indicate the exporter's proforma invoice/quotation number and its date, including item, quantity, price, delivery date, shipping marks, insurance, payment terms documents required, etc. Before acceptance, the export order should he scrutinized in all aspects.

- *Acknowledgement:*

The exporter should write a simple letter to the overseas buyer thanking him for the export order and stating that the confirmation of the same would be sent soon. It may be mentioned here that acknowledgement is different from confirmation.

• *Scrutiny:*

The export purchase order should be examined carefully and its contents scrutinized, in terms of the pro-forma invoice/contract sent to the foreign buyer, on the following aspects.

i) The order has been received for the product for which quotation/offer Was sent and the exporter is still in a position to supply the product.

ii) Size and specifications should be same as per offer/quotation; even slightest variation could create problems for the purchaser and the supplier at a later stage.

iii) Pre-shipment inspection should be either by exporter himself or an agency which is easily available. If the buyer desires the inspection to be done by an agent/agency of his choice, financial and physical aspects of the inspection should be examined and communicated to the buyer. If compulsory pre-shipment inspection by an Indian Export Inspection Agency is required, the buyer should be done at the stage of sending an offer/quotation.

iv) Payment conditions are same as stipulated. An irrevocable Letter Of Credit (L/C) should be opened, where required.

v) Special packaging, labeling and marking requirements, if any, should be noted for compliance. Particular attention should be paid to the individual packaging of consumer goods required for direct sale to the consumers. If such a case, labels, price tags, ploy pack/skin packing etc., would be required and their supply should be assured.

vi) Shipment and delivery date is conformity with the exporters
Production plans and whether:

a) Part shipment is allowed

b) Transhipment is permissible or not

c) Port of shipment/destination is same or changed.

vii) The Documents, which are required with the Bill of Exchange are:

a) Commercial invoice thereon.

b) Certification by an authority on the commercial invoice.

c) Bill of lading 'Straight' or 'to order', 'shipped' or received for shipment', direct or 'through', etc.

d) Certificate of Origin whether the usual one issued by a Trade Association or Chamber of Commerce or special ones like that required for availing of GSP concessions or other preferences.

e) Packing List.

f) Insurance Policy or Certificate.

Confirmation:

If the exporter is satisfied on various aspects referred above, a formal confirmation of the exporter should be sent to the buyer.

Clarification:

If the exporter is not completely satisfied with the terns of the export orde, Clarification should be sought from the buyer before its confirmation.

The clarification could be in terms of quantity, delivery schedule, terms of payment, etc. The delivery Period should be specific and not a value like "immediate delivery" or "as soon as" Possible". Similarly, the payment should be made in the country of the exporter if a foreign bank is involved.

RESERVATION OF SHIPPING SPACE:

• Reservation

If the exporter has accepted/confirmed the export order, his immediate task is to get shipping space reserved in accordance with the delivery Schedule set out therein. Reservation of shipping space commences generally 6 to 8 weeks before the ship's arrival at port. Information on shipping services/sailings can be obtained from the Clearing and Forwarding Agents.

In case the goods are exported by Air, there need not be a reservation of space as it is generally at short notice. However, the exporter must confirm this fact from his Clearing and Forwarding Agent.

• Clearing and Forwarding Agent

The exporter must appoint an agent to help him in the shipment/air freighting of goods,. The clearing and Forwarding Agent should be a firm of repute experienced in handling export/import cargo. If the goods are to be exported by sea, the Clearing and Forwarding Agent should have branches in the major ports like Mumbai, Kolkatta Chennai and Cochin.

DELIVERY NOTE/PURCHASE ORDER

On confirmation of the export order, a delivery note may be issued to be production department or the factory simultaneously in case the exporter has his own manufacturing facility. When the goods are to be procured from other manufacturers/suppliers, a purchase order should be issued by the suppliers.

Contents of the Delivery Note/Purchase Order:-

The Delivery Note/Purchase Order must contain the following details:-

i)   *Details of the Product in terms of :*

    a)   Sizes, specifications, standards, etc.

    b)   Quantity required.

ii) *Delivery schedule:*

The delivery schedule to be indicated to the Production Department or factory of the supplier must be much before the date on which goods are to be shipped, depending upon the time which is spent on transporting the goods from the factory to the port of shipment.

    iii) Any special requirement with regard to the components including raw materials to be used in the product.

    iv)   Packaging/packing stipulations.

    v)   Labelling requirements.

    Forward Exchange Contracts, Export License/Quota, Importer-Exporter Code(IEC) Number, Sales Tax Registration, etc.

On receiving the export order from the buyer, the exporter should get a forward Exchange Contract, Export Licences, central Excice Declaration, Importer Exporter code number (IEC) and Sales tax Registration.

After the receipt of the export order, the following things must be initiated:

a) Forward Exchange Contract:

The exporter should also obtain a Forward Exchange Contract from the banks to cover the risks involved as a result of fluctuation in exchange rate. For obtaining this contract, the exporter should approach his bank along with a

(i)   Application on plain paper for obtaining the Forward Exchange Contract and

(ii)   L/C and/or the Letter of credit.

b) Confirmed Export Order (in original).

The application for the Forward Exchange Contract should clearly indicate the definite period (not the exact date buy period say between such date to such date) in which the export documents would be submitted to the bank. An important condition is that the L/C covering the particular export contract should not be restricted to any bank(s). It must be restricted to the exporter(s) Banks.. On information of the export order, the exporters should ask their overseas customers (importers) to open the L/Cs on their banks.

c) Export Licences/Quota

Incase the product to be exported is subject to the Export Trade Control, the exporter should apply for an Export Licence to the concerned Licensing Authority:

d) Central Excise Declaration

File a declaration with the concerned Central Excise Authority, in case the export goods are subject to Excise Duty and obtain a declarant's Code Number, in case the exporter has not Central

e) Importer-Exporter Code No.(IEC)

Also obtain the Importer-Exporter Code No. from the Regional Licensing Authority concerned.

f) Sales Tax Registration

After the completion of the above said Procedure the exporter should Get registered with the Sales Tax Department and become a Registered Dealer, for obtaining goods without payment of Sales Tax from other manufacturers/merchants.

4.5   THE INTERNATIONAL SALES CONTRACT

The Contract to buy and sell goods is the starting point of international trade. The sales contract includes the transport arrangements, cargo insurance, Customs formalities and payment procedures. Although the contract is central to an international trade transaction, the rules and practice concerning such contracts may very considerably from one export situation to another, depending not only on the legal system involved buy also the type of agreement concluded between the trading partners.

• Offer and Acceptance

An international sales contract comes into being when one party-the exporter –makes an offer and the other – the importer – accepts it. The offer and the acceptance have to match, for the agreement to be formalized. i.e. offer + acceptance = Contract.

• Form of the Contract

Generally the, Export Agreements do not have to follow any particular form, although the precise requirements vary from one country to another. Usually a legally binding contract arises from an agreement between the exporters and the importers. The agreements so formed may be through a format documents, kelexes, and messages through computers, a telephonic conversation or an oral agreement.

• Contents of an Export Contract

The contract should contain

- Specific terms and conditions pertaining to the product/ products that are the subject matter of sale/purchase
- General terms and conditions.

In the first group, Quality and specifications of the product are to be included. These would naturally differ from product to product. What is essential is that in the contract, detailed and carefully description is given about the characteristics, design and specifications of the product. As far as general conditions are concerned, the standardized position can be a good guide, but it is essential that both the exporter and importer do understand the implications of each of the standardized conditions are agree to them in the standardized form after duly considering pros and cons of each one of the conditions.

The important terms & conditions are:

i)   **Formation or conclusion of a contract** In the case of a written agreement, a contract would be deemed to have reached the formation/conclusion stage when both the parties have affixed their signature on it. In the case of a 'construed contract', if one party has sent a telex , telephone or any other kind of message, saying that terms and conditions as referred to in such and such telexes are acceptable. Then the contract would be deemed to have been formed. It is desirable that finally parties exchange reconfirmation messages, as this would avoid all kinds of ambiguities.

ii) **Assignment:** In case the intention of any one of the parties is to assign one's own rights and obligations set out in the contract to some other party, the best course then would be to indicate such arrangement in the contract itself. Unless it is specifically done, there would be difficulties at a later stage.

iii) **Pre-shipment inspection:** It is in the interest of both the parties in a contract, that arrangements of preshipment Inspection of goods for quality, quantity and /or price are mutually agreed upon and incorporated into the contract. This would be helpful at various stages, in particular, in securing payment or making claims on carrier or insurance company. Once the arrangements have been agreed upon and Inspection Agency identified, it is the duty of the exporter, unless a contrary position has been mutually agreed upon by the parties, to inform the agency concerned some days in advance of the date of shipment to take up inspection work. The exporter has to provide all necessary facilities and cooperation to the Inspection Agency. The contract should clearly indicate as to which party is going to bear the cost of inspection – the exporter or importer.

iv) **Product description and specifications** It is the duty of the exporter to ensure that the product is in conformity with the standards and specifications agreed upon. If a sample has been approved by the importer, then the items supplied should match the sample.

v)   Quantity: The contract should indicate in specific terms. If the quantity of goods delivered by exporter is less than the quantity indicated in the contract, the importer then has the right to refuse to take the delivery. However, if the importer does accept short consignment, then he/she is bound to pay for the actual quantity delivered to him/her.

If the consignment is larger than the quantity indicated in the contract, the importer may accept only the quantity contracted and may refuse to accept the excess. However if the importer does accept the excess, then he/she is bound to pay for the excess.

vi)   Quality: The goods delivered by exporter should be in conformity with the contract.

Unless the contract specifically mentions that goods to be supplied may be second hand ones, all supplies have to be of new and of unused goods only.

If the quality of goods is at variance with the contracted quality, the importer can reject the goods and claim damages. Alternatively importer can negotiate with exporter that he would accept goods only if price is reduced by such and such margin.

In situation where exporter is to supply goods in instalments and if more than one instalment is of defective goods, importer has the right to repudiate the whole contract.

vii)   Packing, marking and labeling An export Contract should indicate clearly requirements specially insisted upon by the importer in regard to packing, making and labeling. All the items entail cost, which have to be borne by the exporter who would like to load them on to the quoted price and that is why the entire position in regard to special requirements should be clear from the very beginning. The usual understanding in regard to 'reasonable' packing. In contract to special stipulations set out by importer, is that the exporter shall provide such packing as is required to prevent damage or deterioration of goods during transit to their final destination and that it would be strong and protective enough to withstand, without limitation, rough handling during transit and exposure to vagaries of temperatures, salt and precipitation during transit and open storage. All packages have to be clearly marked and labeled as required in the contract. In the case of marking, information that has to be indicated on each package should be in easily readable ink. Giving the name of the consignee, contents of the package including name of the product, net and sometimes also goods weight, country of origin, etc.

viii) Incoterms, price and total value, the contract should indicate clearly the price and total value. Price would of course, depend upon terms of delivery and for this purpose Incoterms are usually used.

ix) Taxes, duties and other charges that would bear which tax depends very much on how the prices are quoted and herein Incoterms become relevant.

x) **Delivery period** It is important that contracts do clearly indicate stipulations with regard to the delivery period. There should be no vagueness on this issue. Expressions such as immediate', 'prompt', etc. should as far as possible be avoided to describe the delivery

Period, as they give rise to ambiguities. In the case of payment of Letter of Credit (L/C), if the expiry period is expressed in terms of months and not precise dates, the expiry date is determined by taking into account the date on which the exporter received first notification of the L/C either from the issuing or advising bank.

In the case of late deliveries (not involving L/C mechanism of payment), the importer can insist upon payment to be made by exporter by way if liquidated damages, a sum equivalent to a certain percentages of the contract price for every week of delay.

However, acceptance or non-acceptance of late delivery is an option of which only the importer can take advantage. It is perfectly open to the importer not to accept late deliveries at all and exercise the option of rejecting the contract.

xi) **Acceptance** In transactions other than those involving payment by L/C, the importer would be deemed to have accepted goods only when he/she has had reasonable time and opportunity to examine them to determine whether they are in conformity with the contract.

xii) Transfer of risk Incoterms define the point which risk passes on from the exporter to the importer. Unless otherwise agreed between the parties, the risk passes on to the exporter when the goods are handed over to the first carrier for transmission to the importer.

xiii) Mode of payment: The contract should clearly indicate the mode of payment – whether it is L/C or Documentary Collection (D/C) or Document on Acceptance (D/A) – and other precise details, in particular terms, currency, amount etc. in each case.

xiv) Documents It is important that exporter supplies to importer all essential documents pertaining to a contract and its execution. Some important documents being:

- Shipping Advice
- All other essential negotiable and non-negotiable documents, in particular
- Bill of Lading
- Commercial Invoice and its other variations
- Packing list
- Insurance documents
- Certificate of Origin

These documents should be supplied expeditiously. In fact a sound percept is that documents must travel faster than goods.

xv) Guarantees and warranties clause in the contract should clearly provide details of guarantees and warranties and the period over which they will be operative, this clause is usually on the following lines.

"The contractor warrants that everything to be furnished hereunder shall be free from all defects and faults in material. Workmanship and manufacture and is consistent with the established and generally accepted standards for material of the type ordered and in full conformity with the specifications, drawing or samples. The warranty shall apply to inspection of payment for and acceptance of the goods, but shall expire except in respect of complaints notified to the contractor prior to such date, months after their delivery or months after their arrival at the ultimate destination, whichever shall be sooner."

xvi) Redress and liquidated damages: The contract should provide for specific remedies with respect to different contractual defaults, in particular with regard to the quantum and manner of calculations of liquidated damages.

xvii) Force Majeure' and frustration: Sometimes performance of a contract becomes impossible because of occurrence of certain unforeseen and uncontrollable events – e.g. war, civil disturbance, natural calamity, economic upheavals, etc. Such situations are called "Act of God" "Frustrating Events", "Failure of presupposed Conditions: or "Force Majeure".

It is important that Export Contracts contain a clause providing for such eventualities, specifying clearly the type of events that would be covered by the term and if necessary the manner of recognition of such eventualities including, if necessary, remedies and procedures.

International Chambers of Commerce has prepared model contract clauses on "force majeure and hardship". If the intention of the parties of a contract is the ICC model clauses should be applicable to a given contrac t, then they should specifically mention this by suing the following wording.

"The Force Majeure (Exemption, Clauses of the International Chambers of commerce (ICC Publication No.421) is hereby incorporated in this contract.

ICC Publication mentioned above has enumerated the following impediments as the one in respect of which the "force Majeure", clause will be applicable

a) war, whether declared or not, civil war, riots and revolutions, acts of piracy, acts of sabotage;

b) Natural disasters such as violent storms, cyclones, earthquakes, tidal waves, floods, destruction by lightning.

c) Explosions, fires, destruction of machines of factories and of any kind of installations;

d) Boycotts, strikes and lockouts of all kinds, go-slows, occupation of factories and premises and work stoppages which occur in the enterprise of the party seeking relief,

e) Acts of authority, whether lawful or unlawful,. Apart from acts for which the party seeking relief has assumed the risk by virtue of other provisions of the contract;

f) Unless otherwise provided in the contract, impediment does not include lack of authorisations, of licence, of entry of residence permits, or of approvals necessary for the performance of the contract and to be issued by a Public Authority of any kind whatsoever in the country of the party seeking relief.

xviii) **Third party claims and indemnities** If an exporter is supplying some goods or items in which intellectual property rights in the nature of 'patent' or 'copyright' exists, then that fact must not only be disclosed to importer but a suitable clause should be incorporated in the contract. In the absence of such disclosure or clause, the importer would be exempt from any liability or claim made by any third party, in case the importer is required to indemnify the former of all such expenses.

xix) **Settlement of disputes and applicable law** There in indeed no single, uniform, well-integrated and comprehensive International Law which can be applicable to all aspects of international sales contracts. On some specific aspects, however, there are as mentioned earlier. Standard practices and code developed by International Chambers of Commerce, examples being Incoterms, Uniform Customs and Practices for Documentary Credits, etc. If an export contract specifically refers to those standard codes, then provisions as set out in those codes apply. However, if the contracts do not refer to standard codes, nor do they have specific clauses on issues discussed above, then the possibility of difference of opinion leading to dispute may crop up.

SETTLEMENT OF DISPUTES:

For settling disputes one can either go to the Courts of Law, or may choose to resort to Arbitration. It is important that Export Contracts include appropriate clauses indicating how the disputes are going to be resolved.

If any one of the parties decides to go to a Court of Law, then the question arises whether it is the Courts of Law of the exporter's country or those of the importer's country, that have this jurisdiction. The general practice has so far been that, unless in the contract itself the jurisdiction aspect has been clearly spelt out, the law of that country with which the agreement is most closely connected will apply. In the case of an export contract, it is the country of the exporter which is most closely connected with the agreement because it is in that country that the goods are to be assembled and put on board ship and therefore the jurisdiction will be with the exporting country's Courts of Law.

In international trading transactions, parties normally do not like to go to courts and instead decide to go to Arbitration. The fact that disputes are to be settled by resorting to Arbitration should be clearly stated in the contract, inter alia indicting whether Arbitration in accordance with International Chambers of Commerce rules or the rules set out by UN Commission on International Trade Law will be applicable.

4.6   WORLD SHIPPING

Meaning:

Shipping is a physical process of transporting good and cargo, by land, air, and sea. It describes the movement of objects by ship.

Land or "ground" shipping can be by train or by truck. In air and sea shipments, ground transportation is often still required to take the product from its origin to the airport or seaport and then to its destination. Ground transportation is typically more affordable than air shipments, but more expensive than shipping by sea.

Shipment of freight by trucks, directly from the shipper to the destination, is known as a door to door shipment. Vans and trucks make deliveries to sea ports and air ports where freight is moved in bulk.

Much shipping is quote aboard actual ships. An individual nation's fleet and the people that crew it are referred to its merchant navy or merchant marine. Merchant shipping is essential to the world economy, carrying 90% of international trade with 50,000 merchant ships worldwide. The term shipping in this context originated from the shipping trade of wind power ships, and has come to refer to the delivery of cargo and parcels of any size above the common mail of letters and postcards.

PRELIMINARIES:

The procedures for arranging a shipment of goods can be complex. Before goods can be shipped by Sea the exporter or his Shipping or Forwarding Agent must:

- Find out freight rates
- Select a shipping line and a particular vessel
- Book shipping space
- Register cargo on a shipping note and send shipping note to Shipping company
- Register details of Custom entries forms and send to Customs
- Arrange adequate packing, including shipping marks
- Receive calling forward notice from Shipping company
- Send goods to port with consignment note
- Receive Bill of Lading from Shipping company
- Pay freight bill
- Enclose bill of lading and send copies to shipping line and customer, or to the Bank acting as intermediary.

Shipping and Forwarding Agents:

In practice only the largest companies try to handle all the shipping and dispatch of their goods overseas themselves. With large quantities of goods to export they afford to employ their own export staff.

Small exporters feel easier to use the services of Shipping and Forwarding Agents, or freight they are experts on the availability of the different modes of transport for different markets, on the cost, and on the suitability of each mode. Their job involves booking space, arranging documentation and in many cases, collecting the goods from the factory and transporting them to the Docks, Airport, Railway station or Road collection point.

Shipping and Forwarding Agents deal with Customs entries and other formalities. They arrange payment of freight charges and insurance, if necessary and handle collection of necessary documents. They may also help by consolidating or grouping together a number of consignments to make transportation more economic.

Types of Shipping

The freight rates which are to be paid to transport goods by Ocean freight depend to some extent on the type of shipping is used. The four basic types of shipping are:

a) Conference line vessels:

These are ships operated by a line, which is a member of a shipping conference. Conferences are groups of shipping line. They establish common freight rates, regular scheduled departures and common shipping conditions. They provide international liner services for the carriage of Cargo on a specified route or routes.

b) Non-conference vessels:

They are ships operated by shipping companies giving scheduled services but quoting freight rates independently.

c) Tramp ships:

These are ships operated by shipping companies giving scheduled services buy quoting freight rates independently.

d) Charter Ships:

These ships do not follow regular routes but travel as and where cargoes are available.

The most commonly used shipping are Conference Line Vessels, which make regular journeys and offer special discounts to exporters who use them regularly. The exporter or his Freight Forwarder may make such special arrangements with Conference Lines.

The Shipping Company will charge either by weight (W) or measure (M) whichever is greater.

In the case of particularly valuable cargo, the shipping company may charge an ad valorem freight rate. That is an extra charge because the goods are so valuable, such as might be the case with a consignment of furs.

A minimum charge may apply to freight charges if the goods are too small for a Shipping company to handle them strictly by volume or weight.

Freight rates may also be increased by a special surcharge in special situations, such as local unrest or disaster or the need for a longer journey than necessary, as for example, when the Suez Canal was closed. Another possible form of surcharge is after a major devaluation of currency. Or there may be a 'congestion surcharge' which may be as high as 75%.

It is important that these possible 'extras' are taken into account when freight rates are estimated.

Terms of shipment:

The common trading terms used in shipping goods internationally are:

1. Freight On Board, or Free On Board (FOB):

The exporter delivers the goods at the specified location (and on board the vessel). Costs paid by the exporter include load and lash, including securing cargo no to move in the ships hold, protecting, the cargo from contact with the double bottom to prevent slipping, and protection against damage from condensation. For example, "FOP Kunming Airport" means that the exporter delivers the goods to the airport, and pays for the cargo to be loaded and secured on the plane. The exporter is bound to deliver the goods at his cost and expense. In this case, the freight and other expenses for outbound traffic are borne by the importer.

2. Cost and Freight (C&F, CFR, CNF):

Insurance is payable by the importer, and the exporter pays the ocean shipping/air freight costs to the specified location. For example, C&F Los Angeles (the exporter pays the ocean shipping /air freight costs to Los Angeles). Many of the shipping carriers (such as UPS, DHL, and FedEx) offer guarantees on their delivery times. These are known as GSR guarantees or "guaranteed service refunds", if the parcels are not delivered on time, the customer is entitled to a refund.

3. Cost, Insurance, and Freight (CIF):

Insurance and freight are all paid by the exporter to the specified location. For example, at CIF Los Angeles, the exporter pays the ocean shipping/ air freight costs to Los Angeles including the insurance). The term "best way" generally implies that the shipper will choose the carrier who offers the lowest rate (to the shipper) for the shipment. In some cases, however, other factors, such as better insurance or faster transit time will cause the shipper to choose an option other than the lowest bidder.

Shipping component in system begins from outbound delivery creation and supports a lot of functions. The important one's are:

- Picking
- Packing deliveries
- Processing Goods Issue

Picking:

- Picking process involves taking goods from physical storage location and transferring to picking area based on the pick list information, where it would be further processed for packing.

- Picking information on exact quantity is then fed back in system on delivery.

- Picking would be relevant for all materials except materials which are created for services.

- Material is stored in plant in a storage location. In a delivery, to pick the material, storage location should get determined.

- Storage location determination – Rules are defined so that different criteria can be used.

Packing:

Packing is integral part of shipping. When delivery is being processed, delivery items can be selected for packing and assigned to handling units.

- This functionality enables provision of packing information of delivery items to customer & helps in unloading.

- This also helps in updating information on stock of packaging materials for organization allows for representation of multiple levels of packaging.

- Like items packed in box, which is loaded on pallets and then on to truck.

- Items are packed into 'Handling Units' (HU's): Initially empty handling units are created packing screen of delivery into which the materials are packed and information on weight and volumes are fed into it.

- In Standard system material type for packaging materials is "VERP"

- The packaging materials can be added in delivery as an additional item created w/o reference to sales order.

- Provisions are also made in standard system settings to process returnable packaging materials to cater to industry requirements.

Goods Issue:

Immediately after goods leave company, goods issue for the materials needs to be posted in system.

Goods issue has following effect in system:

- Warehouse stock of material is reduced by delivery quantity.

- Value changes are posted to Balance sheet account in inventory management.

- Requirements are reduced by equivalent of delivery quantity.

- Serial number is undated.

- Goods Issue posting is recorded in document flow.

- Update Billing due index for further creation of billing documents.

Goods issue is processed using following options:

- Goods Issue posting for Individual outbound deliveries

- Collective goods issue processing for multiple outbound deliveries in foreground mode.

- Collective goods issue processing for multiple outbound deliveries in background mode.

Tramp Shipping

The term Tramp Shipping refers to chartering of ships on an 'ad hoc' basis. Tramp ships operate in all parts of the world without a fixed shipping route and sailing schedule in search of primarily bulk cargo carried generally in shiploads. Ships are chartered in one or other of the following forms:

a) Voyage Charter:

The ships are chartered for a specific voyage e.g. 10,000m.t, of iron ore from Vizag to Japan. Traders normally opt for this type of charter.

b) Time Charter:

The ships are chartered for a specific period of time, e.g.from 1st January to 31st December of a calendar year. This charter may employ the ship in voyage according to his requirements. The time charterer is a long-term rate, whereas the voyage charter is a short-term rate.

c) Demise Charter:

In both the types of charters mentioned above, the consideration includes the rates for the crew, fuel and other operational requirements, which are provided by the owner of the ship. In the case with floating personnel, fuel and other necessities and operates the ship. Normally a ship owner or prospective ship owner may prefer this method.

4.7   LINERS

Liner Conference

A liner conference is a group of two or more vessel-operating carriers which provides international liner services for the carriages of cargo on a particular route or routes within specified geographical limits on uniform or common freight rates and on other mutually agreed conditions. There are over 360 liner conferences all over the world. The advantages of liner service are that it provides:

a)   Regularity of sailing to scheduled ports of call

b)   Stability of freight rates for a relatively long period of time which enables shippers to quote CIF prices.

c)   Uniform rates for all shippers

d)   Coverage of a wide range of ports, and

e)   Rebates on freight rates based on loyalty arrangements.

Freight Rates

Conference Rate Making: One of the most important activities of a conference is the preparation, publication and revision of conference tariffs. The tariff usually contains a list of rules and regulation regarding proper application of the tariff. Rate-fixation is a complex process, which has to consider factors like character of the cargo, volume of the cargo, its value, availability, distance, packing, susceptibility to pilferage, storage, density, competition, handling costs, insurance charges, direct and indirect costs, fixed costs, port facilities, post regulations, port dues, possibility of return haul etc.

Besides the above, two important factors which always govern the fixation of any freight rate must be considered. They are:

a) Competitiveness and the ability for the cargo to bear the cost on the one hand, and

b) Economic viability of the proposition, from the carrier's point of view, on the other.

Loyalty Arrangements

While the conference specifies the freight rates through rate agreements which specify the conditions under which the signatories to the agreement have to charge the freight rates, "loyalty arrangements" are possible whereby certain rebates can be allowed by the Conference to the shippers for their exclusive patronage of the Conference members. There are three rebate systems in practice for this purpose:

(a) Deferred Payment System:

A shipper who utilizes exclusively the vessels of the member lines of the Conference for the carriage of cargo between the ports covered by the Conference will receive a certain percentage (usually 10%) of his freight payments. The rebate is computed for a designated period called "Shipment Period" which is usually three to six months but is paid after a certain period called "deferred period" of the same duration following the shipment period, on the condition that the shipper has given his exclusive support to the conference lines, both during the shipment period and the deferred period.

(b) The dual rate system:

Shippers who sign an exclusive patronage contract with the conference get the benefit of lower rates compared to those applicable to the shippers who are not on such contracts.

(c) Immediate Rebate system:

In contrast to the Deferred Rebate System, shippers under the Immediate Rebate System are give cash or immediate rebate (usually 9.5%) of freight on payment of freight for their cargoes. This rebate varies from conference to conference.

4.8 TRAMPS

Meaning of tramps:

A tramp is a ship that does not operate on a fixed schedule. They engage in spot freight, picking u contracts as they become available. The terms "tramp', "tramper", and "tramp freighter" are more appropriate today, as very few ocean going vessels of any kind are steamers, and fewer still are tram steamers. The use of the term "tramp" is now way refers to the physical condition of the vessels, although some tramps can be quite run down.

Tramps Today

The general trend in maritime shipping has been toward larger and larger vessels. While the volume of cargo being moved gradually increases, the number of ships carrying them gradually shrinks because the size of the ships is increasing. The only real practical limits on ship size are the widths of the Suez and Panama Canals, as ships too big to use these must take routes that add thousand of miles to their journeys. Container ships, with their mammoth cargo capacity, are rarely employed in the tramp role. However, there tramps drying the sea tanes, especially on shorter routes between minor ports. Both the relatively small tramp freighters and the great container ships often have berths for travelers.

Central Warehousing Corporation

CWC in India is the biggest public warehouse operator having 497warehouse across the country with a storage capacity of 10.3million tones providing warehousing services for a wide range of products ranging from agricultural produce to sophisticated industrial products. Warehousing activities of CWC include food grain warehouses, industrial warehousing, custom bonded warehouses, container freight stations, inland clearance depots and air cargo complexes.

4.9   CONTAINERISATIONS

Containers are super strong steel boxes used to carry cargo aboard ships. Their use has revolutionized the world of international business. Door delivery and pick up using multimodal transportation has been made possible only because of containerization.

Before the invention of containers, cargo used to be shipped in bulk and literally handled by men. These labour-intensive operations often resulted in delays and damages. Containers promised secure and timely delivery of cargo and increased shelf space for perishables due to the climate control possibilities. For containers to work, ship and inland transportation systems around the globe needed modifications. The efficiency and economy by using containers has increased to a great extent.

Container Sizes

TEU – Length – 20' Breath – 8' Height – 8'6" (overall)

FEU - Length – 40' Breath – 8' Height – 8'6" (overall)

In addition, three other lengths 45 ft., 48 ft., and 53 ft. are used internationally. Container capacity (of ships, ports, etc.) is measured in 20-foot equivalent units (TEUs) and 40-foot equivalent units (FEUs).

A standard 20' container has an internal volume of approximately 31 cubic meters and a pay load of 18 tonnes.

FCL – LCL Containers:

Containers can be classified as FCL (Full Container Load) or LCL (Less than Container Load), An FCL originated container arrives at the port fully loaded ready to ship. An LCL shipment arrives as break-bulk cargo (possibly from several different consignors) and has to be stuffed in the container in a groupage shed or Container Freight Station (CFS).

Container Types

* *Insulated Containers:*

Protect against head loss or gain used in conjunction with a blown air refrigeration system to convey perishable or other cargo that needs to be carried under temperature control.

* *Fruit Containers:*

Insulated container with internal dimensions slightly longer.

* *Refrigerated Containers:*

Refrigerated Containers are fitted with their own refrigeration units with an electrical supply for their operation.

- *Bulk Containers:*

Bulk Containers are designed for the carriage of dry powders and granular substances in bulk. To facilitate top loading, three circular hatches (500mm diameter) are fitted in some containers in the roof structure. For discharge, a hatch is fitted in the right hand door of the container.

- *Ventilated Containers:*

Ventilated Containers are of steel construction and have full length ventilation galleries sited along the top and bottom side rails, allowing passive ventilation of the cargo. Ingress of water is prevented.

- *Flat Rack Containers:*

Flat Rack Containers are ideal for uncontainerable cargo.

- *Open Top Containers:*

Open Top Containers have top loading facility suitable where height of cargo is in excess of the height of the standard general purpose container.

- *Half-height Version:*

Half-height Version of the open top container is designed for the carriage of heavy dense cargos such as steel, pipes and tubes etc.

- *Tank Containers;*

Tank Containers generally constructed with the carriage of a specific product or range of products in mind.

- *Open – sided Containers:*

Open – sided Containers accommodates specific commodities such as plywood, perishable commodities and live stock.

- *High Cube Refer:*

High Cube Refer Containers are 12.2mlong, 2.4.m wide and 30m high.

- *Hanger Containers:*

Hanger Containers are used for dry cargo and are equipped with removable beams in the upper part. They are used for shipment of garments on hangers.

- *Bin Containers:*

Bin Containers have no doors are ideal for heavy dense cargos such as steel pipes:

Main maritime routes are composed of oceans, seas, lakes, rivers and channels. However, maritime circulation takes place on specific parts of the maritime space. The Atlantic Ocean is very important since it accounts for 78% of the global trade, 68% of its value and for 75% of the maritime trade. The construction of channels locks and dredging are attempts to facilitate maritime circulation by reducing discontinuity. Maritime transportation has high terminal costs, since port infrastructures are among the most expensive to build, maintain and improve. High inventory costs also characterize maritime transportation. More than any other mode, maritime transportation is linked to heavy industries, such as steel and petrochemical facilities adjacent to port sites.

Water transportation is generally divided into inland waterways (rivers, canals, great lakes). Domestic coastways and seaways. Water transport is resorted to for high bulk, low value commodities because of low cost per tonne kilometer, which is of greater importance than speed of delivery. Basic bulk commodities and raw materials such as iron are, coal, chemicals, petroleum products, cement etc are extensively transported by this mode.

Ships:

There are two kinds of shipping services. The ships that generally operate are the following:

(2)   Liner, and

(3)   Tramp.

The types of ship used are given below:

- Container Ships/box boats
- Tankers
  - Crude Oil
  - Product
  - Chemicals
- Bulk carriers

- General cargo ships
- Cable layers
- Offshore supply vessels
- P (Dynamically Positioned) Ships
- Ferries/RORO (roll on-roll off)
- Gas carriers
- Car Carriers
- Tugboats
- Dredgers
- Barges

Cargo shipment by ships

(a) **General Cargo:** General cargoes are of high value, it does not require any special dimentions. These form the main aspect of international trade. These cargoes are carried generally on liner terms by break-bulk conventional vessels. Developed countries like USA, European countries, Japan etc have recently gone in for untization and pressed unit loaders into service, notably cellular container ships, i.e. ships designed to carry containers, to carry such cargo, because of scarcity of labour and high cost of operation. This is a capital intensive method which increases the productivity and saves costs in the long run, though the initial investment is bound to be heavy for the building of necessary infrastructure, including large container parks, port equipment like gantry cranes, construction of proper roads, strengthening of bridges designing of special rail wagons for inland transport etc.

Containerisation, which comprises 85% of the general cargo market in the world, provides the most cost effective and efficient service and has constantly adapted itself to the needs of the shipping world.

During the 60s and 70s the liner cargo trade was constantly modernized to exploit the economies of scale through high capacity tonnage, resulting in cellular vehicles of various capacities such as 750TEU*s, 1500TUEs, 3000TUEs, 4000TEUs, 6000TEus, For ship owners today containerization is the only means of survival.

*TEU=Ten Equivalent Units

In order to expand their coverage of the world, ship owners are forming global networks called Grand Alliance or mega-carriers combinations such as `six-pack` vessel sharing arrangements between OOCL, APL, Mitsui, Nedlloyd and others. These are done to meet the needs of emerging markets and increasing global customers and competition.

UNIT LOAD

To save time and handling costs, cargoes are consolidated into as large a unit as possible such as 5 tons, 10 tons, 20 tons etc. This helps productivity in cargo handling by displacing labour, which is scarce in certain countries.

CONTAINER

The container is equipment used to store and carry goods. According to the International Organization for Standardisation (ISO) freight container is defined as an article of transport equipment which is:

a)   of a permanent character and can be repeatedly used,

b)   can be carried by one more modes of transport,

c)   Should be fitted with ready handling devices, particularly for transfer from one mode of transport to the other,

d)   Easy to fill and empty,

e)   Have an internal volume of 35.3 cu.ft or more.

There are three types of `classification by use` viz

a)   The General Cargo Container – which does not require temperature control.

b)   The Thermal Containers – which requires refrigerated or insulated storage.

c)   Special Containers – namely bulk containers, tank containers, open top containers, side open containers, flats, car containers, pen containers (to carry livestock)

Principal Factors in Ocean Freight Rates

The principal factors which influence the ocean freight rates are:

a)   A pricing system based on demand.

b)   The rate must be less than the margin between the manufactured cost of the goods and the realizable delivered price at which the good must sold at the destination.

c)   The competitive situation facing the conference.

d)   Cost of ship operation.

e)   The transport quality relating to the density of the commodity.

f)   The distance will not be dominant in rate making, as the bulk ocean transportation cost in incurred in loading.

Freighting of containerised cargo

Usually there are three types of freighting arrangement they are:

a)   Commodity Box Rates

This is the most popular form of freighting. Normally 20ft container is taken as freighting unit. It is normally stuffed with similar products. But if the commodity is different, freight will also be different.

b)   Freight All Kinds (FAK)

The carrier quotes an amount per 20ft container, irrespective of what is stored. The shipper uses this for cargoes which give him freight advantages.

c)   Conventional Tariff Rates for Less than Container Load cargo

When shippers have limited qualities of cargo, the carriers accept them as they are and issue separate bills of lading. These are received at the destination by the carrier`s representatives who delivers them to the respective consignees against the bills of ladings.

CONTAINERISATION IN INDIA

Containerisation was first introduced in India by the Indian Railways in 1966. (A brief history of containerization the world over has been discussed at the beginning of this chapter.) The concept of sea containers was first introduced in India in 1968 at a seminar held by the National Ship owners` Association. Though Cochin Port received containers for the first time, India seriously started to adopt containerization in 1978 in major ports like Bombay, Coching, Madras, Haldia/Calcutta. Inland Container Deports (ICDs) – also called dry ports where shipping formalities can be completed for containerized cargo instead of in the exit gateway port. ICDs in India carry out several functions such as stuffing, destuffing, locking, sealing providing trailers, chassis, railway flats, repair handling equipment, storage facilities for reefer, customs examination and processing of customs documents, issuance of combined transport documents by carriers.

Inland Container Depots in India

The following depots have been set up to serve shippers and consignees located at inland centers:

Location	Established
Bangalore	August 1981
Guntur	April 1983
Anaparti	April 1983
Coimbatore	December 1983
Delhi (Pragati Maidan)	March 1984
Delhi (Tuglakabad Softcoke siding)	February 1985
Amingaon (Guwahati)	November 1985
Ludhiana	August 1986

Container Corporation of India Ltd:

The objective of the Container Corporation of India Ltd, (Concor) constituted on March 1, 1998, was to organizee multimodal transport logistics to facilitate the nation`s foreign trade.

Container terminals operated by CONCOR are as under:

NORTHERN INDIA	SOUTHERN INDIA	EASTERN INDIA
Delhi	Tondiarpet (Chennai)	Cossipur
Moradabad	Bangalore	Shalimar
Panipat	Coimbatore	Amingaon (Assam)
Ludhiana	Milavittan	
Agra	Cochin	

WESTERN INDIA	CENTRAL INDIA
Ahmedabad	Hyderabad
Kandla	Guntur
Wadi Bunder	Anaparti
Mulund	Chirala
New Mulund	

These terminals handle both international and domestic traffic. A part from using ISO containers, CONCOR has introduced containers especially for domestic traffic.

The Government of India has broken the monopoly of state-owned Container Corporation of India (Concor), which hauls containers by rail from inland container depots (ICDs) to port across the country.

Export and Import Procedures at ICDs

Exports:

Exporters will have to submit the following documents:

- Five copies of shipping bills at the inland container depots
- Mention the port of exit and the serial numbers of the containers.
- Full set of GR-1 (Guarantee Remittance) form
- Invoices and container wise packing list/weight specifications indicating number of packages, net weight in each container along with the corresponding shipping bill number

Import at Gateway Port

Once the container is unloaded at the port of entry, the particulars of the container should be checked with the sub-manifest, which should be earlier submitted in duplicate by the shipping agent, and the container secured with customs seal.

On arrival of the containers at the ICD, the particulars of the containers, seals etc shall be checked against the transshipment permit received after the endorsement of the transshipment permit.

Cargo Consolidation

Consolidation is an essential faculty for shippers/consignees of small parcels. A consolidator collects consignments from different small shippers, negotiates with line operators and arrives at rates normally offered to large-scale regular clients.

1) Benefits of consolidation to the exporters and shippers.

- Cost advantage
- Door-to-door transportation and distribution services
- Consolidator takes care of arranging in-land transportation.
- The consolidator monitors the cargo movement and informs the shipper
- In case of cargo claims the shipper has to deal only with the consolidator and not with different carries transporting his cargo.

2) To freight forwarder

The forwarders usually benefit financially to the extent of the difference between the total freight charges on the individual consignments paid by the discounted freight which he has to pay to the carrier for the consolidated consignment.

3) To the carriers...

- There is considerable savings in paperwork and time, as there is no handling of individual cargo.
- It saves on expenditure which he would have otherwise incurred in maintaining freight handling equipment and in emplaying workers to handle LCL, shipment.
- There is no risk of freight payments by the individual shippers and this is taken care of by the freight forwarder.

The scope in India for consolidation is enormous as the country has great potentials for export. All exporters do not get large volume of export orders and small size of shipments become a problem for them.

Loss Prevention Measures

Types of damages/losses

Major damages/losses incurred by containerized cargoes are:

- Water damage (fresh or salt water or both)
- Sweat damage , including mould damage
- Damage resulting from breakdown or inadequacy of refrigeration equipment
- Breaking, crushing or other damage due to inadequate packing.
- Damage from overheating or freezing of the container contents
- Breaking, crushing or other damage due to bad stowage.
- Contamination (due to incompatibility of goods stowed in the same container)
- Theft and pilferage.
- Damage or loss from failure of ships fittings, gear, or impact with another container or cargo

Preventive Measures

Proper and timely attention to following can avert or minimize the loss or damages:

- Condition of the container.
- Packing of goods.
- Stowing goods in the container.
- Stowing the container aboard ship.
- Equipment for handling the container(construction of the container in relation to equipment handling)
- Sealing and protection of the container.
- Instructions to forwards (consolidators)
- Documentation
- Terminal operation

The exporter or consigner, or whoever loads the goods, should carefully inspect the condition of the container and recorded the faults noted by inspection on the bill of lading.

Adequate attention should be paid to packing of goods, or they may not reach the destination in good order or condition. The packing must be able to withstand thee effect of the adverse environment. Shippers in their own interest should not economize on packing. The consignment suffers damage due to inadequacy in packing against transportation hazards.

Insurance of Container and Cargo

Insurance companies in India still do not provide full insurance cover for containerization and multimodal transport. For marine insurance there are different premium rates for conventional/break-bulk cargo for inland as well as international transit. In order to lodge a claim with the insurance company, following have to be taken into account:

- Marine Insurance can be taken for c.i.f. value of the goods plus 10% (Total 110%)

- The insured should notify the insurer about suspected loss/ damage following which the insurer appoints a surveyor.

- After receipt of the survey report, a claim has to be filed on the insurer and following document has to be submitted in respect of overseas shipment.

- Evidence of insurance - Original copy
- Evidence of shipment - Copy of bill of lading, Parcel Way Bill/Receipt, Consignment Note/ Airway Evidence of Value Copy of Invoice
- Evidence of Loss - Survey report or short landing Certificate
- Letter of Subrogation
- Notices/correspondence with carrier
- Claim Bill

Claim bill has to cover the following:

a) Actual claim calculated on the basis of survey report for insured Value.

b) Survey fees.

c) In respect of short-landing, insured value of short landed packages.

Container Insurance

Insurance coverage of container is based on period with a duration of one year as a rule (called "floater contract").

A voyage wise insurance policy "trip contract" is also available, which is normally for less than a year.

CONTAINER LEASING – METHODS AND ORGANIZATION

Leasing of containers has become widespread owing to the huge initial investments required for containerization.

Leasing:

Containers are taken on lease by carries from container manufactures or owners. There are four types of leasing arrangement:

a)   Trip lease or short term lease,

b)   Long-term lese (3years to 5 years)

c)   Financial Lease – a hire – purchase or installment purchase scheme,

d)   Master Lease – a deal between ship owner and leasing company for 1-2 years wherein the ship owner guarantees a container leasing company that a minimum numbers of containers will always be under his lease.

Advantages of using leased containers

a)   Avoids tying up of funds, thereby avoiding large expenditure at one time. Leasing allows the company to use the container only on payment of a fixed lease rate.

b)   Avoids depreciation: Containers are owned by leasing companies and are to be depreciated by them.

c)   Avoids risks of having obsolete facilities: leasing enables the owner to return unnecessary vehicles and avoid the risk of obsolescence.

d)   To enable coping with regional or seasonal fluctuations in the number of containers required and also to save positioning costs.

e)   To save storage charges while idling as the containers can be procured for the shortest possible period needed, which may be profitable.

f)   To lessen the burden of maintenance or control jobs.

g)   To avoid the effects of inflation as the rental charges are fixed to cover the entire period.

Disadvantages of Leasing

a)   No residual value to the lessee at the end of the long-term lease.

b)   Leasing cost is high. When a container is leased for its entire economic life span, the lease payment must cover the following costs of the lessor:

    i)   Costs of purchasing container.

    ii)   Interest paid on the original financing or opportunity cost of the capital tied up in the container.

    iii) A portion of the lessor`s overhead cost of doing business.

    iv)   Lesser profit.

Basic Types of lease contract

a) Trip Lease :

When a user needs and takes a container case by case, he may go in for

• **One way lease:**

Where the user takes the container whenever he needs them and return them thee destination the leasing company.

• **Round-trip lease:**

Where the origin and the destination are the same. Containers have to be returned to the origin.

b) Rate agreement:

This is a type of trip-lease with a fixed rental charge. The charge would not vary principles of demand and supply. But under this contract the lessor is obliged to supply containers to the extent that they are available at that time.

c) Master Lease:

The Master Lease obligates the user to lease a certain number of containers during the period of the contract only.

d) Long –Term Lease:

Under this contract specified containers are leased for a certain period. Inter-change of containers is not allowed and the user is obliged to continue using the same containers throughout the contract period.

CONTAINER HANDLING SYSTEMS AND EQUIPMENTS

The most commonly used container handling methods in operation are:

a) Trailer Storage System:

The import containers discharged from a ship by crane are placed on a road trailer, which is towed to an assigned position in the storage area where it remains until collected by a road tractor. These are then placed in the storage area and then towed to the ship by port equipment.

b) Straddle-Carrier System:

Straddle carries can stack containers two or three high, move them between them to or from road transport. The straddle carrier is widely used, which is a testimony to its flexibility and its ability to meet peak requirements.

c) Gantry Cranes System:

In this system containers in the storage area are stacked by rail-mounted or rubber-tyred gantry cranes. Rail mounted cranes can stock containers up to five high, while the rubber-tired do go up to two to three high.

d) Mixed System:

Mixed system employs the best equipment for the particular operation. However, for such systems to be successful, a comprehensive information system and rigid operating policies are required, together with excellent management.

e) Types of Container Handling Equipment:

The large size of ISO containers necessitates large equipment for handling.

h) Gantry-Cranes :

Gantry-Cranes are specially designed for container traffic. A mobile gantry-crane is basically a gantry-crane on rubber tyres, which combines the mobility of straddle-carriers with the wide spans and height of gantry-cranes.

i) Computerized Communication and Information:

Containerisation can be efficient only if the operation are computerized. Private sector can take a lead in providing these services by establishing computer/EDI/internet centers and maintaining them efficient.

j) Fork-lift trucks:

Fork-lift trucks can be used for container handlings, but not all containers have fork tunnels. Most operators, therefore, equip their fork-lift trucks with high level spreader - beams as well. Side-loading trucks designed for container handling lift the container form
the ground or from a truck or stack, move it horizontally and place it on the wide platform for stability.

f) Inland Transport Equipment:

Road chassis or road trailers could be flat bed or of skeletal type. The containers are fixed with pinlocks which are also called twist locks. During pickups and deliveries the containers are under revenue load, otherwise this are dead mileages. When a rod tractor moves without trailer attached, this is bob sailing Railroads, or railways also have flat beds or skeletal wagons.

MARITIME FRAUDS AND CONTAINER CRIMES

Types of Frauds

1. Documentary Frauds:

Some or the entire document specified by the buyer for presentation by the seller to the bank to receive payment are forged.

2. *Shipping Frauds:*

> Scuttling, deviation, cargo theft, arson or staged accidental fires in which vessel or cargo is disposed off with the convenience of the owners.

3. *Charter Party Frauds:*

> When one or two contracting parties default leaving the other to clear the mess

4. *Container crimes:*

> Though containerization has resulted in considerable reduction in theft and pilferage, entire containers are often found to be stolen. This is an increasing concern to the operators of container terminals, the places where such thefts are most likely to occur.

Security Sealing:

The sealing system is very important as is the selection of the seal. The purpose of the seal is to indicate continued integrity and immediate evidence of tampering.

Agents for General Insurance:

Risks involved in container operations are covered by Insurance Companies, Protection and Indemnity Clubs and Though Transport Clubs of intermediaries. Agencies of these organizations can be taken private companies and individuals.

Claim Consultancy Service and Other Professional Legal Services:

Private agencies or individuals can take up jobs of consultancy, claim adjusters and claim processors.

Chapter-V

5.1 EXPORT PROMOTION MEASURES

INTRODUCTION:

Assistance to States for Development of Export Infrastructure and Allied Activities (ASIDE) Scheme. In pursuance of the EXIM Policy announcement in March, 2000, the ASIDE scheme was launched on 13.3.2002.

The basic objectives of the Scheme are:-

- To involve the States in the growth of export i. by providing incentive-linked assistance to the State Governments.
- To create appropriate infrastructure for the development and growth of exports.

Prior to the launch of ASIDE scheme, the Department Of Commerce (DoC) had been implementing four infrastructure development schemes viz. the Export Promotion Industrial Park Scheme (EPIP), Export Promotion Zones Scheme (EPZ), the Critical Infrastructure Balancing Scheme (CIB) and the Export Development Fund (EDF) for the North-East and Sikkim. The new Scheme subsumed the aforementioned ongoing Central Schemes in order to give a boost to development of export related infrastructure.

ASIDE is a Centrally Sponsored Plan scheme. It provides outlay for development of export infrastructure, which is distributed among the States, inter alia, on the basis of the States' export performance in the previous year.

The outlay of the scheme has two components: 80% of the funds (State component) are earmarked for allocation to the States on the basis of the approved criteria. The balance 20% (Central component), and amount equivalent to un-utilized portion of the funds allocated to the States in the past year(s), if any, is retained at the Central level for meeting the requirements of inter-state projects, capital outlays of SEZs, activities relating to promotion of exports from the North Eastern Region as per the existing guidelines of the Export Development Fund and any other activity considered important by the Central Government from the regional or national perspective.

At the Central Level, an Empowered Committee under the chairmanship of the Commerce Secretary with representatives of other Departments, approves and monitors the projects under the Central Sector. This Empowered Committee also periodically reviews the progress of the scheme and takes steps to ensure achievement of the objectives of the scheme. At the State Level, a State Level Export Promotion Committee (SLEPC) headed by the Chief Secretary of the State and consisting of the Secretaries of concerned Departments at the State level, a representative of the States Cell of the Department of Commerce (DoC), the Joint Director General of Foreign Trade posted in that State/ region and the Development Commissioner of the SEZ's in the State scrutinizes and approves specific projects and oversees the implementation of the scheme.

The funds are disbursed directly to a Nodal Agency nominated by the State Government where it is kept in a separate financial head in the accounts of the Nodal Agency. The specific purposes for which the funds can be sanctioned and utilized under the Scheme as per the approved criteria are:

- Creation of new Export Promotion Industrial Parks/Zones (including Special

  Economic Zones (SEZs)/Agri-Business Zones) and augmenting facilities in the

  Existing Zones.

- Setting up of electronic and other related infrastructure in export enclaves.

- Equity participation in infrastructure projects, including the setting up of SEZs.

- Meeting the requirements of capital outlay of EPIPs/SEZs.

- Development of complementary infrastructure such as roads connecting the production centers with ports, setting up of Inland Container Depots and Container Freight Stations.

- Stabilizing power supply through additional transformers and islanding of export production centers, etc.

- Development of minor ports and jetties of a particular specification to serve exports.

- Assistance for setting up Common Effluent Treatment Plants.

- Projects of national and regional importance.

- Activities permitted as per the Export Development Fund in relation to the North East and Sikkim.

    Rs.2, 050 crore was spent under this scheme during the 10th Five Year Plan (2002-2007). During the 11th Five Year Plan, an outlay of Rs.3,793 crore was approved for the Scheme. The allocation for financial year 2010-11 is Rs.662.98 crore.

Outlay and Sanctions/Releases under ASIDE (Value in Rs. Crore)

Year	Total Outlay	Sanction/ Release to States (including N.E. Region	Sanction/ Release in the Central Sector	Total Sanction/ Release under ASIDE
2002-03	325.46	241.00	84.46	325.46
2003-04	350.00	252.00	98.00	350.00
2004-05	424.88	313.84	111.04	424.88
2005-06	500.99	383.00	117.99	500.99
2006-07	450.00	358.92	90.25	449.17
2007-08	569.00	439.99	129.01	569.00
2008-09	570.00	437.84	131.40	569.24
2009-10	570.00	433.93	136.07	570.00
2010-11	662.98	400.00	75.59	475.59*

Assistance to States for Developing Export Infrastructure and Allied activities (ASIDE) Scheme

Year-wise allocations/releases of funds to the States/UTs under State Component of ASIDE Scheme (Rs.crore)

(Rs. in Crore)

State	2002-03		2003-04		2004-05		2005-06		2006-07	
	Outlay	Release	Outlay	Release	Outlay	Release	Outlay	Release	Outlay	Release
Andhra Pardesh	12.00	12.00	13.00	13.00	13.85	13.85	15.45	15.45	17.00	8.50
Andaman & Nicobar Islands	2.00	2.00	2.00	1.00	2.00	0	2.00	0	2.20	0
Bihar	3.00	3.00	6.50	0	2.00	0	2.00	0	2.00	0
Chandigarh	1.00	1.00	2.00	0	2.00	0	3.20	3.20	3.50	1.75
Chhattisgarh	4.00	4.00	4.00	4.00	5.00	5.00	5.00	5.00	5.00	5.00
Dadra & Nagar Haveli	1.50	1.50	3.00	0	2.00	0	2.00	0	2.00	0
Daman & Diu	1.50	1.50	3.00	0	2.00	0	2.00	0	2.00	0
Delhi	1.00	1.00	2.00	0	2.65	0	2.65	2.65	2.90	1.45
Goa	6.00	6.00	6.00	6.00	3.73	3.73	6.09	6.09	6.70	0
Gujarat	14.00	14.00	15.00	15.00	35.78	35.78	43.38	43.38	47.70	47.70
Haryana	6.00	6.00	6.00	6.00	8.49	8.49	14.05	14.05	15.45	7.725

State										
Himachal Pradesh	7.00	7.00	7.50	7.50	5.00	5.00	5.53	5.53	6.00	3.00
Jammu & Kashmir	6.00	6.00	6.00	6.00	5.00	5.00	5.25	5.25	5.80	2.90
Jharkhand	4.00	4.00	4.00	4.00	5.00	0	5.00	0	5.50	2.75
Karnataka	18.00	18.00	19.00	19.00	24.14	24.14	33.99	33.99	37.40	18.70
Kerala	11.00	11.00	12.00	12.00	9.30	9.30	10.69	10.69	11.75	5.875
Lakshadweep	2.00	2.00	2.00	2.00	2.00	0	2.00	0	2.20	0
Madhya Pradesh	20.00	20.00	11.00	11.00	14.35	14.35	14.35	14.35	15.80	7.90
Maharashtra	16.00	16.00	34.00	34.00	57.09	57.09	65.52	65.52	72.10	72.10
Orissa	4.50	4.50	10.00	10.00	6.05	6.05	6.93	6.93	7.65	7.65
Pondicherry	3.00	3.00	3.00	1.50	2.00	0	2.00	0	2.20	0
Punjab	9.00	9.00	10.00	10.00	9.68	9.68	12.17	12.17	13.4	6.70
Rajasthan	12.00	12.00	13.00	13.00	13.20	13.20	13.20	13.20	14.53	7.265
Tamil Nadu	28.00	28.00	30.00	30.00	39.19	39.19	39.19	39.19	43.12	43.12
Uttar Pradesh	20.00	20.00	21.00	21.00	12.59	12.59	21.00	21.00	23.10	11.55
Uttaranchal	4.00	4.00	4.00	2.00	5.00	5.00	5.27	5.27	5.80	0
West Bengal	10.00	10.00	11.00	11.00	14.91	14.91	20.09	20.09	22.10	22.10
Total	226.50	226.50	260.00	239.00	304.00	282.35	360.00	343.00	396.00	284.235

State	2002-03		2003-04		2004-05		2005-06		2006-07	
	Outlay	Release	Outlay	Release	Outlay	Release	Outlay	Release	Outlay	Release
Arunachal Pradesh	1.00	1.00	1.25	1.25	2.51	0	2.51	2.51	2.76	0
North Eastern Region										
Assam	4.00	4.00	5.00	5.00	11.49	11.49	12.57	12.57	13.83	0
Manipur	2.00	2.00	2.50	0	2.00	2.00	2.06	2.06	2.07	2.27
Mizoram	1.00	1.00	2.50	0	2.00	2.00	3.24	3.24	3.56	1.78
Meghalaya	2.00	2.00	2.50	2.50	5.72	5.72	8.34	8.34	9.17	9.17
Nagaland	1.00	1.00	1.25	0.50	2.00	2.00	2.00	2.00	2.20	1.10
Sikkim	0.50	0.50	1.25	0	2.00	0	2.00	2.00	2.20	1.10
Tripura	3.00	3.00	3.75	3.75	8.28	8.28	7.28	7.28	8.10	4.005
Total	14.50	14.50	20.00	13.00	36.00	31.49	40.00	40.00	44.00	19.425
Grand Total	241.00	241.00	280.00	252.00	340.00	313.00	400.00	383.00	440.00	303.66

(Rs. in Crore)

Year	Total Outlay	Releases to state (including N.E Region)	Releases in the Central Sector	Total Releases under ASIDE
2002-03	325.46	241.00	84.46	325.46
2003-04	350.00	252.00	98.00	350.00
2004-05	424.88	313.84	111.04	424.88
2005-06	500.99	383.00	117.99	500.99
2006-07	550.00	303.66	70.03	373.69
(as on 8.1.07)	450.00(RE)			

Upgradation of road and rail stretches constituting back linkages to the ICPs are being taken up on top priority.

Infrastructure Support:

The Government facilitates transport/logistic support and resolves problems experienced by the trading community in the carriage of goods by courier, sea, air, rail and road in coordination with the concerned Ministries and Departments. It seeks to encourage greater containerization, computerization of cargo clearance and electronic data interchange, warehousing, setting up of air cargo complexes, inland container depots, container freight stations, etc. As a result of these efforts, export and import have been facilitated through various orders of the Government. The airlines/other carriers having annual transshipment volume above 2500 MT to/from any airport, the same would be exempt from Bank Guarantee for carriage of goods on transshipment. Further, the jurisdictional Commissioners of Customs in deserving cases may also consider giving waiver of bank guarantee. There has been a constant endeavor to solve the problem of congestion in handling and clearance of containers at the Jawaharlal Nehru Port and the Inland Container Depot, Tughlakabad. An Action Group on Trade Facilitation has been formed to recommend simplification of customs procedures leading to reduction of dwell time in cargo clearance.

Single window clearance for proposals for setting up of Inland Container Depots/Container Freight Stations/Air Cargo Complexes (ICDs/CFSs/ACCs) is implemented through an Inter-Ministerial Committee (IMC) since 1992. So far, 28 proposals for setting up Inland Container Depots/Container Freight Stations (ICDs/ CFSs) and Air Cargo Complexes (ACCs) have been approved by the IMC.

Two high level committees viz. the Standing Committee on Promotion of Exports by Sea (SCOPE-SHIPPING) and the Standing Committee on Promotion of Exports by Air (SCOPE-AIR) have been set up to address the constraints in smooth movement of international cargo and resolve problems of exporters concerning Customs, Containerisation, Air, Shipping, and Railways related issues. The meetings of these two committees were held in Chennai in January, 2006.

Electronic Data Interchange (EDI) is also being implemented in a phased manner at Ports and Airports so as to facilitate electronic clearance of export and import containers.

Market Access Initiative (MAI) Scheme

The Market Access Initiative (MAI) Scheme is a plan scheme to act as a catalyst to promote India's exports on a sustained basis. The Scheme is based upon 'focus product' and 'focus market' concept. Under the Scheme, assistance is extended to the Departments of Central Government and organizations of Central/State Governments, Export Promotion Councils, Registered Trade Promotion organizations, Commodity Boards, Recognized Apex Trade Bodies, Recognized Industrial Clusters and individual Exporters (only for product registration and testing charges for engineering products abroad). Assistance is given for the following components:

Market studies

Marketing projects which may include:

1.   Opening of showrooms
2.   Warehousing facility
3.   Display in international departmental stores
4.   Publicity campaign
5.   Participation in trade fairs, BSMs etc., abroad

6. Research and product development

7. Reverse visits of the prominent foreign buyers etc. from the project focus counties

- Export potential survey of the States
- Registration charges for product registration abroad for Pharmaceuticals, Biotechnology and Agro-Chemicals.
- Testing charges for Engineering products abroad
- Cottage and Handicrafts units for similar activities and for developing the web site for virtual exhibition.
- Studies on WTO related matters
- Industrial clusters for marketing studies, participation in trade fairs etc.

Additional Activities included in the MAI Scheme

- National Level Participation & Organizing Trade Festival of India, BSMs abroad.
- Publication of World Class Catalogues
- Publicity Campaign and Brand Promotion
- Research and Product Development
- Assistance for up-gradation of Laboratories, in Universities, Research Institutions, National Level Institutions for fulfilling Sanitary and Phyto Sanitary (SPS) measures related testing
- Capacity building of exporters for export related matters and product up-gradation
- Developing Common facility Centers, Design Centers etc.
- Hiring consultant/designers in the prospective/buyer country
- Anti Dumping, Anti Money Laundering and other investigations/compliances.
- Studies on WTO related matters and JSG/FTA/RTA Studies
- Project Development

New Agencies eligible under MAI Scheme

- Indian Missions
- National Level institutions like IITs, IIM, NIDs, NIFT etc

- Research Institutions, universities and recognized laboratories

  Any project/study which the Empowered Committee feels would further the objectives of the Scheme.

The Scheme has been revised during the current year by adding of more activities relating to marketing projects, capacity building, support for statutory compliance, studies and project development etc. and more agencies have been made eligible for assistance under the scheme.

Details about outlays during 2002-2007 and actual expenditure are given below: (Rs. Lakh)

Year	Budget	Actual
2002-03	4200	1086
2003-04	4400	900
2004-05	10244	484
2005-06	4000	1991
2006-07	4000	2669
		(up to December)

Marketing Development Assistance (MDA)

To facilitate various measures being undertaken to stimulate and diversify the country's export trade, Marketing Development Assistance (MDA) Scheme is under operation in the Department of Commerce. The Scheme supports the under mentioned activities:

- Assist individual exporters for export promotion activities abroad.

- Assist Export Promotion Councils (EPCs) to undertake export promotion activities for their product(s) and commodities

- Assist approved organizations/trade bodies in undertaking limited exclusive non-recurring innovative activities connected with export promotion efforts for their members.

- Assist Focus Area export promotion programmes in specific regions abroad like Focus LAC, Focus Africa, Focus CIS and ASEAN+2 programmes.

- Promote residual essential activities connected with marketing promotion efforts abroad.

Eligible Agencies

• Recognized Export Promotion Councils (EPCs).

• Exporting companies with an f.o.b. value of exports of upto Rs.15.00 crore in the preceding year

• Export Promotion Agencies like ITPO, FIEO, KVIC

Details about outlays during 2002-2007 and actual expenditure are given below: (Rs. Lakh)

Year	Budget	Actual
2002-03	4500.00	4484.91
2003-04	5200.00	5200.00
2004-05	5500.00	5500.00
2005-06	5500.00	3847.00
2006-07	5225.00(RE)	3113.00
		(up to December 2006)

During the year 2006-07, the Indian Oilseeds and Produce Exporters Association (IOPEA) was approved as an Export Promotion Council for the De-oiled Cake and meals, Oilseeds and Edible Oils other than those dealt by Shellac EPC. Khadi and Village Industries Commission (KVIC) has been accorded a deemed EPC status and will be extended assistance on the pattern of an umbrella EPC like FIEO. KVIC's proposals for participation in International Fairs, organizing BSMs etc. would be approved, as per admissibility under MDA/MAI guidelines. J&K Chamber of Commerce was also assisted for the first time to participate in International Fairs/exhibitions under MAI scheme.

Export Credit Guarantee Corporation of India Limited (ECGC)

The Corporation was established in 1957 as the Export Risk Insurance Corporation Limited. Keeping in view the wider role played by the Corporation, the name was changed to Export Credit Guarantee Corporation of India Limited (ECGC). The ECGC is the premier organization in the country, which offers credit risk insurance cover to exporters, banks, etc. The primary objective of the Corporation is to promote the country's exports by covering the risk of export on credit. It provides (a) a range of insurance covers to Indian exporters against the risk of non realization of export proceeds due to commercial or political causes and (b) different types of guarantees to banks and other financial institutions to enable them to extend credit facilities to exporters on liberal basis.

Achievements of ECGC during 2005-06

Transfer guarantees are issued to banks in India which add confirmation to letters of credit and such guarantees protect banks against loss that may be sustained due to default of banks are certain political risks. The total value of shipment declared under the scheme amounted to Rs. 37590.19 crore as compared to Rs. 35,987.01 crore in 2004-05 recording a growth of 4.45 per cent,

The total premium income during the year amounted to Rs. 577.33 crore as compared to 515.54 crore in 2004-05 registering a growth 11.99 per cent. The amount contributed to growth came from short term guarantee business which amounted for 67.25 per cent of the total premium income followed by short term policy sector including factoring which contribute to 28.28 per cent. Income from medium and long term sector amounts to Rs. 25.79 crore which is 4.47 per cent of the total premium income.

The total gross income of the Corporation amounted to Rs. 705.48 crore compared to Rs. 591.07 crore for the previous year. The premium income was Rs. 543.05 crore against Rs. 476.13 crore for the previous year. Other income for the year was Rs. 162.44 crore as against Rs. 114.05 crore for the previous year.

The total expenditure came to Rs. 362.91 crore comprising of Rs. 249.63 crore by way of net claims paid and provisions for liability, Rs. 113.28 crore being administrative expenditure and write offs including depreciation. The year ended with a profit of Rs. 343.57 crore before tax as compared to Rs. 119.51 crore for the previous year.

The Corporation declared and paid a dividend of Rs. 45.35 crore for the year 2005-06 as compared to Rs. 15.23 crore for the previous year.

National Export Insurance Account (NEIA):

A separate Fund with a corpus of Rs. 2,000.00 crore called the National Export Insurance Account (NEIA) was set up with the approval of the Cabinet Committee on Economic Affairs (CCEA) in its meeting held on 24.01.2006. The objective of NEIA is to promote project exports from India, which may not take place but for the support of a credit risk insurance cover in the following cases:

- High risk on a single country
- High value of a single transaction
- Large valued projects involving unusual or unconventional credit terms, which are beyond the normal, risk bearing capacity of ECGC.
- The progress achieved during the current year is given below:
- The NEIA Trust was registered with an initial corpus of Rs. 66 crore under Bombay Public Trust Act, 1950 on 8th May, 2006.
- The second installment of Rs. 180 crore was received on 10th October, 2006 taking the total amount of funds to Rs. 246 crore. The Corpus is expected to be enhanced to Rs. 2000 crore by the end of the 11th Plan period.
- Projects fulfilling following criteria will receive NEIA support:
  1. The project by itself should be commercially viable.
  2. The project should be strategically important for India, with regard to the economic and political relationship of India with the project country.
  3. The exporter should be capable of executing the contract, as evident from his previous track record.
  4. ECGC is not able to cover the project on its own, due to its underwriting constraints.
- TCIL's Angola Project has been approved in principle provided Government of India backed Line of Credit to Angola does not materialize. The value of the Angola project is US$ 10 million. Other projects are under consideration.

India Brand Equity Foundation (IBEF)

The India Brand Equity Foundation is working as a public-private partnership with the Confederation of Indian Industry. The activities undertaken by the IBEF during the year are given below:

- "India Everywhere" campaign was successfully launched at the Annual Meeting of the World Economic Forum in Davos,

Singapore at the "Celebrating India in Singapore Week" and "Hannover Fair".

- The IBEF's partnership with the World Economic Forum was carried forward and extended to initiatives in the markets of China and Japan.

- Organized an Indo-German Business Summit at Hannover. Over the following months, business audiences across markets to Japan, UK, Belgium, China, Brazil and Italy were engaged.

- Show cased a business exhibition at the European Parliament in Brussels on contemporary India.

- Business seminars were organized in collaboration with Ministry of Finance during the 39th Annual Meeting of the Board of Governors of ADB held in May, 2006 in Hyderabad and India Economic Summit held in November, 2006 in New Delhi.

  The film titled "Young and Resurgent India" was screened on a gratis basis by BBC World, Doordarshan, Aaj Tak, Zee and CNN IBN channels.

- sIndian economic studies on States of India were prepared highlighting the business trends and key opportunities.

- Engaged with academic delegations as well as international journalists from across markets USA, Sweden, Brazil, Brussels, Germany, Italy and South Africa. Prominent among the former were inter-actions with the Kellogg School of Management, Dakin University, Stockholm University School of Business, Babcock School of Business.

- Developed a website for the Ministry of Finance to promote investment in infrastructure projects in India. The website was launched on December 21, 2006.

5.2 TRADE FINANCE

Trade Finance coordinates the pre-budget proposals received from Apex Industry Associations/Chambers of Commerce, Export Promotion Councils, Commodity Boards, Federation of Exporters' Organizations, individuals companies, etc. The Department through the Export-Import Bank of India and in line with the trading opportunities proactively endeavored to enhance the competitiveness of Indian exporters while also striving to ensure that Banks' activities and financing initiatives keep pace with the discerning requirements of industry and trade. Taking into consideration our trading requirements, the Department has taken up the matter with the Ministry of Finance for opening new branches or upgrading the status of the existing branches of Indian Banks abroad and of Foreign Banks in India.

At the initiative of the Department, the RBI has taken the decision to continue the existing Rupee Export Credit Interest Rates up to 30 April, 2007 with a view to assist the exporters. With a view to help the exporters, representations/complaints involving export credit/exchange control matters were also taken up with the Ministry of Finance and the Reserve Bank of India. A Working Group consisting of the RBI, select banks and export organizations was set up in April, 2005 on export credit.

The function of this group is to review

(i)   Action taken on exporters' satisfaction survey,

(ii) Existing procedures for export credit,

(iii) Gold Card Scheme,

(iv) Export credit for non-star exporters, and

(v)   The current interest rate regulations in export credit. The Working Group had recommended several measures to improve customer service. In the light of the recommendations, RBI has issued instructions to banks; the important ones are given below:

Review of the existing procedure for export credit

1.   There is a need for attitudinal change in the approach of banks' officials in small and medium exporters. Banks may take suitable steps in this regard.

2. Banks should put in place a control and reporting mechanism to ensure that the applications for export credit especially from Small and Medium Exporters are disposed of within the prescribed time frame.

3. Small and Medium Exporters especially in the upcountry centers should be properly trained by SSI/export organizations with technical assistance from banks regarding correct filling up of forms.

State Level Export Promotion Committees (SLEPCs) which have been reconstituted as sub-committees of the SLBCs should play a greater role in promoting coordination between banks and exporters.

Review of the Gold Card Scheme

1. Since the number of Gold cards issued by banks is low, banks were advised to speed up the process of issue of the Cards to all the eligible exporters especially the SME exporters.

2. Simplified procedure for issue of Gold Cards as envisaged under the scheme should be implemented by all banks.

Review of export credit for non-star exporters

Banks should post nodal officers at Regional / Zonal Offices major branches for attending to credit related problems of SME exporters.

Review of other issues

1. The interest rates prescribed by RBI are ceiling rates. Since the banks are at liberty to charge lesser rates of interest, banks may consider extending export credit at rates lesser than the ceiling rates prescribed by RBI.

2. Banks should give priority for the foreign currency export credit requirements of exporters over foreign currency loans to non-exporter borrowers.

Interest on export credit in Foreign Currency

1. As recommended by the Working Group the ceiling rate of interest on export credit in foreign currency by banks was revised to LIBOR plus 100 basis points w.e.f. April 18, 2006 from the existing ceiling rate of LIBOR plus 75 basis points.

eTrade Project:

The community project `eTrade' is being pursued in various trade regulatory and facilitating agencies like Customs, DGFT, Ports, Airports, RBI, Export Promotion Organisations (EPO), Exporters, Importers, Agents, CONCOR and Banks. The objectives of this project are to facilitate electronic delivery of services; to simplify procedures; to provide 24 hour access to users with their partners; to make procedure transparent; to reduce the transaction cost and time and to introduce international standards and best practices.

The project has witnessed good progress over the year and one of the major achievements was operationalisation of web based system for electronic interface between Airports Authority of India and importers, exporters, airlines, agents etc. All export transactions are done through this system at the airports of Delhi, Chennai, Mumbai and Kolkata. The import cycle is also being streamlined. Similarly CONCOR has operationalised the web based system for e-filing of documents by its community partners at Tuglakabad. The electronic data interchange (EDI) system for express courier is under development. The Department organized the 9th United Nations Centre for Trade Facilitation and Electronic Business (UN/CEFACT) Forum meeting from 2-6 October, 2006 along with the United Nations Electronic Trade Document (UNeDocs) workshop from 3-4 October, 2006 at New Delhi. This was attended by around 275 participants from twenty eight countries around the world. The focus of the five day event was the development and simplification of electronic data interchange, e-business and administrative processes in most of public and private sectors such as finance, health, business, environment, and so on.

Important Initiatives taken by EPCs

With a view to boost exports, the government provides various incentives and promotional schemes through its Commodity Boards/Councils for infrastructure development, quality and quality control, market development and promotion, packaging, publicity, information dissemination etc. Some of the initiatives undertaken are given as under:

Shellace & Minor Forest Produce

With a view to strengthen the backward linkages for exports, the Shellac EPC is undertaking projects on expansion of cultivation of several Minor

Forest Produce (MFP) including Lac, Guar, Cheronjee, in existing areas and extension of their cultivation to new areas as well. To generate employment and income from these activities at grass root level, the Council aims at forming 5,300 SHGs in 8 MFP producing States, in association with respective State governments, and with fund support from various centrally sponsored schemes like Swarnajayanti Gram Swarojgar Yojana (SGSY). The Department of Rural Development has given in-principle approval to the following 4 special projects:

- Proposal for Guar Swarojgar Program in Haryana, Rajasthan, and Gujarat. The project aims at increasing 50 per cent guar seed production and guar gum export in 5 years, providing income of Rs. 15,000 per Beneficiary per year.

- Proposal for Lac Swarojgar Program in West Bengal, Orissa, Andhra Pradesh and Chattisgarh. The project aims at increasing lac production and Shellac exports by 2011, providing income of Rs. 15,000 per Beneficiary per year.

- Proposal for Lac Swarojgar Programme in Patalkot and Chhindwara areas of Madhya Pradesh. The project aims at increasing the lac production by 4.75 lakh kgs in India by 2011, providing income of Rs. 14,500 per Beneficiary per year.

- Proposal for Cheronjee Swarojgar Programe in Amarwara region of Chhindwara district of Madhya Pradesh. The project aims at increasing Cheronjee production by 1000 MT in India by 2011, providing income of Rs. 11,000 per Beneficiary per year.

As part of its mission of enhancing Industry competency and spinoff benefits of employment generation amongst weaker sections of society attached with MFP, SHEFEXIL has also undertaken the second step by initiating a pilot project successfully in Lac cultivation in Purulia, which is the Lac growing district in West Bengal. It is targeted to benefit 600 SHGs in Purulia, in association with Department of Panchayats and Rural development, Government of West Bengal. Out of this, the Council has already helped set up 300 SHGs in the area, most of which are run by women. It has already set up a Broodlac Farm, in that area.

Engineering Exports

The Engineering Export Promotion Council (EEPC) had released funds for various export promotion activities such as holding buyer-seller meets, organizing and participating in exhibitions abroad, conducting market surveys and for providing services to exporters of engineering products through its offices abroad, etc. under the General and Focus Area Program. During 2006-07, the EEPC organized the following important events:

- Hannover Fair, Hannover, Germany April 24-28
- India Pavillion at INTERPHEX, Singapore June 27-29
- Automechanika Frankfurt September
- 2-17
- India Pavillion at SAITEX, Johannesburg October 10-13
- INDEE Cairo November 23-26

The India Pavillion at the Hannover Fair 2006 was jointly inaugurated by Dr. Manmohan Singh, Hon'ble Prime Minister of India and Dr. Angela Merkel, Hon'ble Chancellor of Federal Republic of Germany on 23rd April, 2006. 315 Indian entrepreneurs, both from PSUs and Public Sector, showcased the advancement of Indian technology. Besides, there was state level participation from Governments of West Bengal, Orissa, Jharkhand, Gujarat and Karnataka. A series of Business Summits, Conferences and Seminars were organized during the exhibition. A Memorandum of Understanding (MoU) was also signed between EEPC and German Engineering Federation (VDMA) on 27th April to promote business trade between India and Germany.

The Indian Engineering Exhibition (INDEE) was held in Cairo, Egypt from 23rd to 26th November 2006. INDEE-Cairo opened a new vista in trade relations between the two countries and has provided an ideal platform for exporters of engineering products and services to address the highly potential and ever-growing market of Egypt, Middle East and other North African (MENA) region. Major exhibits on display in INDEE included automotive components, hand tools, cutting tools, pharmaceutical machinery, electrical appliances, fasteners, pumps, diesel engines, gears & gear boxes, castings & forgings, stainless steel utensils, railway track fitting etc.

Gems and Jewellery

Gems & Jewellery has been identified as a thrust sector in the Foreign Trade Policy. The Annual Supplement to the Foreign Trade Policy issued on 7th April, 2006 has extended the following facilities to this sector:

(i)   Import of gold of 8 carat and above has been allowed under the replenishment scheme subject to the import being accompanied by an Assay Certificate specifying the purity, weight and alloy content.

(ii) Duty Free import entitlement of consumables for metals other than Gold, Platinum to be 2 per cent of FOB value of exports during the previous financial year.

(iii) Duty free import entitlement of commercial samples to be Rs. 300,000.

(iv) Duty free re-import entitlement for rejected jewellery to be 2 per cent of the FOB value of exports.

(v)   Cutting and polishing of gems and jewellery, to be treated as manufacturing for the purposes of exemption under Section 10A of the Income Tax Act.

(vi) Import of precious metal scrap / used jewellery has been allowed for melting, refining and re-export of jewellery. However, such import will not be allowed through hand baggage.

(vii) Gem & Jewellery exporters have been allowed to export jewellery on consignment basis.

(viii) Gem & Jewellery exporters have been allowed to export cut and polished precious and semi-precious stones for treatment and re-import.

(ix) Value addition norms for different categories of gems and jewellery products have been reduced.

Kimberley Process Certification Scheme:

The Kimberley Process Certification Scheme (KPCS) is an international certification scheme aimed at preventing conflict diamonds from entering the legitimate trade, from funding conflicts and from fueling human rights abuses, in terms of UN resolution No.55/56 (2000). At present KPCS has 71 Member-States (including EU). India is one of the founding members of the KPCS. India has been unanimously selected as Vice-Chair for the year 2007 in the Plenary of KPCS held in Botswana in November 2006. India will automatically assume Chair of the JPCS in January, 2008 for a period of one year.

During the year 2006-07, the Gem and Jewellery Export Promotion Council (GJEPC) participated in various exhibitions in India and abroad given as below:

- International Jewellery Tokyo (IJT) 2006, Tokyo, Japan
- Vicenza Oro 1 at Vicenza, Italy
- Bangkok Gems and Jewellery Fair, Bangkok, Thailand
- Hong Kong International Jewellery Show 2006, Hong Kong
- OROGEMMA 2005, Vicenza, Italy
- Jewellery Arabia 2005, Bahrain
- The Council promoted the image of Indian gem and jewellery products abroad in print media through release of advertisements and organized India International Jewellery Show (IIJS) 2006 in Mumbai
- During 2006, India participated in Inter-Sessional and Plenary Meetings of Kimberley Process Certification Scheme (KPCS) 2006 in Gaborone, Botswana.

Services Exports

In order to give proper direction, guidance and encouragement to the Services Sector, the Government on the recommendations of a Task Force constituted in this regard has announced setting up of an exclusive Export Promotion Council for Services (SEPC). The Government has initially identified the following 11 services sectors being supported through the SEPC:

- Health Care Services,
- Educational Services;
- Entertainment Services;
- Consultancy Services;
- Architectural Services/Interior Decoration;
- Distribution Services;

- Accounting/Auditing and Book Keeping
- Maritime Transport Services;
- Marketing Research & Management Services;
- Printing and Publishing
- Legal Services

5.3 EXPORT HOUSES, TRADING HOUSES, STAR TRADING HOUSES AND SUPERSTAR TRADING HOUSES

Objective:

The objective of the scheme is to recognize established exporters as Export House, Trading House, Star Trading House and Super Star Trading House with a view to building marketing infrastructure and expertise required for export promotion. Such Houses should operate as highly professional and dynamic institutions and act as important instruments of export growth.

Eligibility

Merchant as well as Manufacturer exporters, Service providers, Export Oriented Units (EOUs)/ units located in Export Processing Zones (EPZs)/ Special Economic Zone (SEZ's) /Electronic Hardware Technology Parks (EHTPs)/ Software Technology Parks (STPs) shall be eligible for such recognition.

Criterion for Recognition

The eligibility criterion for such recognition shall be on the basis of the FOB/NFE value of export of goods and services, including software exports made directly, as well as on the basis of services rendered by the service provider during the preceding three licensing years or the preceding licensing year, at the option of the exporter. The exports made, both in free foreign exchange and in Indian Rupees, shall be taken into account for the purpose of recognition.

Exports made by Subsidiary Company

The exports made by a subsidiary of a limited company shall be counted towards export performance of the limited company for the purpose of recognition. For this purpose, the company shall have the majority share holding in the subsidiary company.

Calculation of Net Foreign Exchange

For the purpose of calculation of the Net Foreign Exchange earned on exports, the value of all the licenses including the value of 2.5 times of the DEPB Credit earned/ granted and the value of duty free gold/ silver/ platinum taken from nominated agency or from foreign supplier shall be deducted from the FOB value of exports made by the person. However, the value of freely transferable SIL, EPCG licenses and the value of licenses surrendered during the validity of license shall not be deducted.

Weightage to exports

For the purpose of recognition, weightage shall be given to the following categories of exports provided such exports are made in freely convertible currency:

Triple weightage on FOB or NFE on the export of products manufactured and exported by units in the Small Scale Industry (SSI)/ Tiny sector/Cottage Sector and double weightage on FOB or NFE to merchant exporter exporting products reserved for SSI units and manufactured by units in the Small Scale Industry (SSI)/Tiny sector/ Cottage Sector. The facility under this paragraph shall not be available to units exporting gems & jewellery products.

- Triple weightage on FOB/NFE on the export of products manufactured and exported by the handlooms and handicraft sector (including handloom made silk products), hand knotted carpets, carpets made of silk and double weightage on FOB/ NFE to merchant exporter exporting products manufactured by the handlooms and handicraft sector (including handloom made silk products), hand knotted carpets, carpets made of silk

- Double weightage on FOB or NFE on the export of fruits and vegetables, floriculture and horticulture produce/ products, project exports.

- Double weightage on FOB or NFE on export of goods manufactured in North Eastern States;

- Double weightage on FOB or NFE on export to such The manufacturing units registered with KVIC or KVIBs shall be granted triple weightage on FOB or NFE on the export of products manufactured and exported by them with effect from 15th August, 97. However, such units shall not be entitled for the weightage given in sub paragraph (a) and (b) above.

- Double weightage on FOB or NFE on exports made by units having ISO 9000(series) or IS/ISO 9000 (series) or ISO 14000 (series) certification.

- Double weightage on FOB or NFE on exports of bar coded products

- Double weightage on FOB or NFE on export of goods manufactured in Jammu and Kashmir.

Recognition for State Corporations

With a view to encouraging participation of State Governments and Union Territories in export promotion, one state corporation nominated by the respective State Government/Union Territory may be recognized as an Export House, even though the criterion for such recognition is not fulfilled by it. This benefit shall be available only for such period and in accordance with such terms and conditions as may be specified from time to time.

Validity Period

Status Certificate shall be valid for a period of three years starting from 1st April of the licensing year during which the application for the grant of such recognition is made, unless otherwise specified. On the expiry of such certificate, application for renewal of status certificate shall be required to be made within a period as prescribed. During the said period, the status holder shall be eligible to claim the usual facilities and benefits, except the benefit of a SIL.

Facilities

All status holders shall be entitled to such facilities as specified in chapter-12

Transitional Arrangement

Status holders shall continue to hold the recognition accorded to them for the period for which such recognition was accorded.

Manufacturing Companies/Industrial Houses

Manufacturing companies or Industrial houses with an annual manufacturing turnover of Rs.300 Crores and Rs.1, 000 Crores in the preceding licensing year shall be recognized as Star Trading House and Super Star Trading House respectively on signing a Memorandum of Understanding in the prescribed form for achieving physical exports as currently prescribed for these categories over a period of next three years. Similarly, companies/project exporters, domestic service providers with annual turnover of Rs.100 Crores or more in the preceding licensing year shall be recognized as Export House and International Service Export House respectively on signing a Memorandum of Understanding in the prescribed form for achieving physical exports as currently prescribed for this category over a period of next three years. Service providers shall be entitled to recognition as Service Export House, International Service Export House, International Star Service Export House, and International Super Star Service Export House on earning free foreign exchange as given in paragraph 15.7 of the Policy.

Golden Status Certificate

Exporters who have attained Export House, Trading House, Star Trading Houses and Super Star Trading Houses status for three terms or more and continue to export shall be eligible for golden status certificate which would enable them to enjoy the benefits of status certificate irrespective of their actual performance.

LERMS

The partial convertibility of the rupee introduced in the budget of 1992 which is also referred to Liberalized Exchange Rate Management System is a very significant move and one can consider it as an export incentive.

According to this 40% of the foreign exchange earned by an exporter is converted at the official RBI rate, and 60% is converted at a —Market Determined Rate, Which is bound to be higher. The 40% of the exchange surrendered to the RBI and converted at the official rate will be used for import of essential items such as petroleum products, fertilizers, defense expenditure and life saving drugs.

This new system completely replaces the old — Replenishment License and later Exim Scripts issued by the Government for exporters, because the premium on the 60% surrendered at market rate would be the incentive. Further, for all allowable imports, importers will have to approach the bank and get import licences cut market rate the total volume of the imports will be automatically regulated by the available volume of foreign exchange. Scarcity of foreign exchange will be reflected in a premium which will accrue to exporters, thus providing a built-in incentive to increase the flows. Hence, it will be appropriate to call LERMS as an export incentive. Perhaps this is the only important export incentive left. The very negotiation of the export documents through the bank will help, realize this incentive.

5.4 EXPORT ORIENTED UNITS (EOU)

Government of India is taking various export promotion measures. It is relevant here to recollect about Free Trade Zone (FTZ) of Export Processing Zone (EPZ) several concessions are given to the units in these zones and it was started from 1965. It was restricted to certain specific areas (like backward areas) and they were given concessional space, building etc. the number of EPZ did not increase much and therefore to complement the efforts of EPZ, EOU (Export Oriented Units) were approved in 1980-81.

These units can be started anywhere in India on the basis of export promotion facilities available in the place. Though EOU's are not getting space at concessional rate, the EOU's are eligible for many other benefits:

- Duty Free imports of capital goods, raw material, components
- Concession in central excise and other central levies, sales tax, corporate income tax.
- More liberal foreign collaboration terms.
- Export finance at concessional rate of interest
- Supply of goods to another 100% EOU is considered as deemed export.
- Can export their goods through Export Houses/Trading houses etc.
- 25% of the production can be sold in the DTA (Domestic Tariff Area)
- Foreign Direct Investment permitted upto 100%

- Can have private bonded warehouse
- Priority in giving telephone, telex.
- Can operate foreign currency account in bank
- Can get MDA
- Can insure with ECGC
- Can open overseas offices
- Self certification of preshipment inspection permitted
- Can send representatives on foreign delegation

INFRASTRUCTURE FACILITIES

The exporters are provided with infrastructural facilities in the following areas:

- Air transport
- Ocean Transport and Containerization
- Rail Transport and
- Power

Air Transport

The infrastructural ground handling facilities and air cargo services are considered for efficient transportation. Some of the measures taken in this activity are Air Cargo complexes have been set up in the gateway airports of Delhi, Mumbai and Chennai. Such facilities are provided in inland airports of Bangalore, Ahmadabad, Hyderabad, Trivandrum, Varanasi, Jaipur, Srinagar, Cochin, Amritsar. It is possible to have air cargo booking, pre-shipment in section and customs clearance from these airports.

In order to assess and monitor backlog of cargo to gateway airports, and to provide additional services through sectional flights Monitoring cells have been established. 40 to 50% of freight rate can be discounted for fresh fruits and vegetables to Gulf countries and for leather exports to European countries.

Varying specific commodity rates of discounts have been notified for garments, carpets, drugs, pharmaceuticals, opium mica, chemicals, toys, games, athletic and sports goods, news paper, magazines, periodicals, printed materials, handicrafts and data processing equipment for different destination. These facilities help to export goods with ease and to get the financial concessions through discounts.

Ocean transport and containerization

Facilities provided in this field are:

- Export Promotion Councils (EPC) has provided Export Cargo projections to the shipping sector.

- The problems of port using exporters are smoothly solved by co-ordination with the Ministry of Surface Transport, Major port trust, and EPCs.

- The Export documentation formalities are completed under one roof by setting up Export Documentation centre (EDC) at the ports of Chennai and Kolkata.

- The cost for standard services in the shipyards has been streamlined to avoid unnecessary dispute and delay.

- Continued efforts are taken through Working Group of the Ministry of Surface Transport to simplify the procedures, reduce handling charges and to improve handling facilities.

Rail Transport

The major facilities provided apart from the general facilities for parcel/goods through trains to the ports and neighboring countries have been sorted out by mutual discussions by the Ministry of Railways and Ministry of surface Transport.

Wagon allotments are made on preferential basis for movement of export goods by rail.

Power

Measures have been taken to provide supply of power without power cut or disruption for the export industries. So also, steps have been taken to provide continued supply of diesel oil at comparable international price to the units exporting 25% or more of the production.

Conclusion

Infrastructure facilities are essential for speedy and efficient movement of the export goods. Since time is cost in any business, more so in export business, any amount of delay will drastically affect the export trade.

OTHER INCENTIVES AND FACILITIES

The Govt. of India is providing several other incentive and facilities to promote export trade. Some of them are:

- (a)   Buyer-Seller Meet
- (b)   Export awards
- (c)   Export training
- (d)   Foreign travel to study of the market
- (e)   Foreign exchange facilities
- (f)   Insurance Risk Cover
- (g)   Relaxation of MRTP Act
- (h)   Research studies
- (i)   Subsidies
- (j)   Tax Concessions
- (k)   Technology and capital goods facilities
- (l)   Trade Fairs and Exhibitions
- (m)   Air Freight subsidy
- (n)   Facilities offered by Spices Board
- (o)   Facilities by APEDA/MPEDA

(a) Buyer-Seller Meet

The Trade Development Authority (TDA) organizes such meets to help the exporters to get better contacts. The objectives of Buyer-Seller meet are.

- •   To know the demand for our products
- •   To familiarize importers on the quality and range of materials available in India
- •   To identify areas of capacity creation, product development, adaptation, improvement in quality control and sales techniques

- To establish market contacts and booking spot orders
- To generate enquires for Indian products

(b) Export Awards

Exporters with outstanding export performance are awarded with certificates of merit and trophies, to encourage them by giving due recognition. These awards are given even for small scale sector also. Some of the criteria applied to select the best awardees on an objective basis are: Development of new markets abroad for products of India

Substantial increase in it exports of non-traditional and finished products Successful introduction of new products in the export market Product development Breakthrough in difficult markets abroad.

(c) Export Training

Training the exporters and their personnel is an important step to promote export. Then only they will know the latest trends in export market and the methods and techniques adopted by developed countries for the export promotion.

(d) Foreign Travel

Such orientation tours are organized by the IIFT and ITC especially in respect of select non-traditional products. The exporters and their personnel visit important foreign market and study the needs of such markets. This enables them to plan their products to suit the needs of such markets, understood through such study tours. They are permitted to book orders when they are on study tour also.

(e) Foreign Exchange Facilities

Forex is provided upto certain limits to the exporters for maintenance and other purposes when they visit foreign countries for export promotion, trade fair etc.

Blanket forex permit is also issued by RBI to firms earning forex for more than Rs.10lakhs and consultants earning Rs. 5 lakhs or more.

(f) Insurance Risk Cover

Risk cover upto 90% is given by ECGC for political, commercial and other risks. There are other special schemes also.

(g) Relaxation on MRTP

Big industrial houses or allowed to enter the middle sector, of they agree to export atleast 75% of their production export sales will be excluded to compute its dominance. In allowing automatic expansion of a dominant undertaking, consideration would be given for its previous export performance.

(h) Research Studies

Research Studies are undertaken by specialized export supporting agencies like IIFT, TDA, Export Promotion Council, Commodity Boards. There are general studies and specific studies on specific products in specific markets abroad.

(i) Subsidies

In order to make Indian Commodities competitive in the world market, subsidies are given. For example freight subsidy is given mostly to goods transported by air (leather goods). MDA subsidy is another form of subsidy.

RBI gives subsidies to Commercial Banks and Exim Bank to certain lines of credit.

(j) Tax Concessions

Tax concessions are given for export of technical know-how in technical service. Dividend Royalty, fees etc received on such service are exempted from tax. There are tax concessions for maintenance of office/agency outsides India, presentation of tenders and the expenditure to prepare them, distribution expenses outside India etc.

(k) Technology and Capital Goods

Import of technology and capital goods for export production are allowed freely by the Government. Imports of spares, equipment and components are also permitted subject to certain conditions. Export Houses, Trading Houses etc. are permitted to import design, drawings and other documents for manufacturing export goods.

(l) Trade Fair and Exhibitions

Trade Fair and Exhibitions in India and abroad provide excellent opportunity for export promotion informing the interested importers the availability of products, their quality, and utility.

The Trade Fair Authority of India (TFAI) co-ordinates such activities and invites registered firms and export houses to participate in the fairs.

Subsidized participation charges on freights, insurance, handling, forwarding and clearing charges, construction of stands, publicities are available to participants in all such fairs and exhibitions.

(m) Air Freight subsidy on Horticulture and Floriculture Exports

The Agricultural and Processed Foods Exports Development Authority (APEDA) provides air freight subsidy on selected fruits, vegetables and floriculture products exports from India.

(n) Facilities Offered by the Spices Board.

The spices Board provides various facilities for the marketing of spices to the exporters having Spice House certificate or Spices board Logo are eligible for the grant of financial assistance for various export promotion activities. Rates have been fixed for different activities like, product promotion, printing brochures packaging, sending samples (air freight), ISO 9000 Technology transfer and R&D.

(o) Facilities by APEDA

The APEDA provides financial assistance for the development and promotion of export of agricultural, horticultural and meat product. Packaging Development, Quality Control Assistance, Upgradation of Meat Plants, Organization building and Human Resource Development.

The Marine products Export Development Authority (MPEDA) provides financial assistance to the exporters of marine products under the following schemes. Infrastructure Development, Prawn farming, Diversification and Modification, Quality Control, Marketing Services.

Products Coverage and Rates

The various items eligible for air subsidy are as follows:

Fresh fruits:

Mangoes other than alphonso, banana, strawberries, papaya, Watermelon

Fresh Vegetables:

Asparagus, Brocolli, Mashroom

Floriculture products:

Cut flowers, live plant/bulbs, gladiolus and other live plants. Rates of subside, Conditions, Applications are prescribed.

The financial assistance rates have been fixed by APEDA / MPEDA is in the nature of reimbursement of expenses incurred by the export firms registered with these agencies.

5.5 SPECIAL ECONOMIC ZONES (SEZ)

Scheme

This may be called the Special Economic Zones Scheme

Definitions:

For the purpose of Special Economic zone scheme, unless the context otherwise requires, the following words and expressions shall have the meanings attached to them as given in the policy.

Eligibility

Special Economic Zones (SEZ) are growth engines that can boost manufacturing, augment exports and generate employment. The private sector has been actively associated with the development of SEZs. The SEZs require special fiscal and regulatory regime in order to impart a hassle free operational regime encompassing the state of the art infrastructure and support services. Special Economic Zones (SEZ) are duty free enclaves which are set up separately from the DTA, for the purpose of low cost production of goods meant for export, provided with facilities like infrastructure, machinery, customs, expertise, etc.

Goods and services going into the SEZ area from Domestic Tariff Area (DTA) shall be treated as export and goods coming from the SEZ area into DTA shall be treated as export and goods coming from the SEZ area into DTA shall be treated as if these are being imported.

Activities in a SEZ?

1. SEZ units may export goods and services including agro-products, party processed goods, sub-assembling and components except prohibited items of exports in ITC (HS). The units may also export by products, rejects, waste scrap arising our of the production process. Export of Special Chemicals, Organisms, Materials, Equipment and Technologies (SCOMET) shall be subject to fulfillment of the conditions indicated in the ITC (HS) Classification of Export and Import items. SEZ units, other than trading/service e unit, may also export to Russian Federation in Indian Rupees against repayment of State Credit/Escrow Rupee Account of the buyer, subject to RBI clearance, if any

2. SEZ unit may import/procure from the DTA without payment of duty all types of goods and services, including capital goods. Whether new or second hand, required by it for its activities or in connection therewith. Provided they are not prohibited items of imports in the ITC (HS). However, any permission required for import under any other law shall be applicable. Goods shall include raw material for making capital goods for use within the unit. The units shall also be permitted to import goods required for the approved activity, including capital goods, free of cost or on loan from clients.

3. SEZ units may procure goods required by it without payment of duty, from bonded warehouses in the DTA set up under the Policy and/or under section 65 of the Customs Act and from Internationals Exhibitions held in India.

4. SEZ units may import/ procure from DTA, without payment of duty, all types of goods for creating a central facility for use by units in SEZ. The Central facility for software development cal also is accessed by units in the DTA for export of software.

5. Gem & Jewellery units may also source gold/silver/platinum through the nominated agencies.

6. SEZ Units may import/procure goods and service from DTA without payment of duty for setting up, operation and maintenance of units in the Zone.

Leasing of Capital Goods

SEZ units may, on the basis of a firm contract between the parties, source the capital goods from a domestic/foreign leasing company. In such a case the SEZ unit and the domestic/foreign leasing company shall jointly file the documents to enable import/procurement of the capital goods without payment of duty.

Net Foreign Exchange Earning (NFE)

SEZ unit shall be a positive Net foreign Exchange Earner. Net Foreign Exchange Earning (NFE) shall be calculated cumulatively for a period of five years from the commencement of production.

Monitoring of performance

The performance of SEZ units shall be monitored by the Unit Approval Committee.

The performance of SEZ units shall be monitored as per the guidelines

Legal Undertaking

The unit is required to execute a legal undertaking with the Development Commissioner concerned and in the event of failure to achieve positive foreign exchange earning it shall be liable to penalty in terms of the legal undertaking or under any other law for the time being in force.

Approvals and Application

Applications for setting up a unit in SEZ other than proposals for setting up of unit in the services sector (except software and IT enabled services, trading or any other service activity as may be delegated by the BOA), shall be approved or rejected by the Units Approval Committee within 15 days as per procedure.

Proposals for setting up units in SEZ requiring Industrial Licences may be granted approval by the Development Commissioner after clearance of the proposal by the SEZ Board of Approval and Department of Industrial Policy and Promotion within 45 days on merits.

DTA Sales and Supplies

SEZ unit may sell goods, including by procedure, and ω service in DTA in accordance with the import policy in force, on payment of applicable duty. DTA sale by service/trading units shall be subject to achievement of positive NFE cumulatively. Similarly for units undertaking manufacturing and services/trading activities against a single LOP. DTA sale shall be subject to achievement of NFE cumulatively.

The following supplies effect in DTA by SEZ units ϖ will be counted for the purpose of fulfillment of positive NFE:

- a. Supplies effect in DTA

- b. Supplies made to bonded warehouses set up under the policy and/ or under Section 65 of the Customs Act.

- c. Supplies to other EOU/SEZ/EHTP/STP/BTP units provided that such goods or   services are permissible to be procured/rendered by these units.

- d. Supplies against special entitlement of duty free import of goods.

- e. Supplies of goods and service to such organizations which are entitled for duty free import of such items in terms of general exemption notification issued by the Ministry of Finance.

- f. Supply of service (by service units) relating to exports paid for in free foreign exchange or for such service rendered in Indian Rupees which are otherwise considered as having been paid for in free foreign exchange by RBI.

- g. Supplies of Information Technology Agreement (ITA-I) items and notified zero duty telecom/electronic items.

Inter-unit Transfer and Other Entitlements

SEZ units may transfer manufactured goods, including ϖ party processed/ semi finished goods and services from one SEZ unit to another EOU/ SEZ/EHTP/STP unit.

Goods imported/procured by a SEZ unit may be transferred or given on loan to another unit within the same SEZ which shall be duty accounted for, but not counted towards discharge of export performance.

Capital goods imported/procured may be transferred or given on loan to another EOU/SEZ/EHTP/STP unit with prior permission of the Development commissioner and Customs authorities concerned.

Transfer of goods in terms of sub-Para (a) and (b) above within the same SEZ shall not require any permission but the units shall maintain proper accounts of the transaction.

Sub Contracting

SEZ unit may sub contract a part of their production ᴆ or production process through units in the DRA or through other EOU/SEZ/EHTP/STP, with the annual permission of Customs authorities. Sub-contracting of part of production process may also be permitted abroad with the approval of the Development Commissioner.

All units, including gem and jewellery, may sub-contract part of the production or production process through other unites in the same SEZ without permission of Custom authorities subject to records being maintained by both the supplying and receiving units.

Exit from SEZ Scheme

SEZ unit may opt out of the scheme with the approval of the Development Commissioner. Such exit from the scheme shall subject to payment of applicable Customs and Excise duties on the imported and indigenous capital goods, raw materials etc, and finished goods in stock. In case the unit has not achieved positive NFE, the exit shall be subject to penalty, which may be imposed by the adjudicating authority under Foreign Trade (Development and Regulation) Act, 1992.

SEZ unit may also be permitted by the Development Commissioner, as one time option, to exit from SEZ scheme on payment of duty on capital goods under the Prevailing EPCG scheme, subject to the unit satisfying the eligibility criteria of that scheme and standard conditions.

Personal Carriage of Export/Import Parcel Import/export through personal carriage of gem and jewellery items may be undertaken as per the procedure prescribed by Customs, Import/export through personal carriage for units. Other than gem and jewellery unit, shall be allowed provided the goods are not in commercial quantity.

Export/Import by post/Courier

Goods including free samples may be export/imported by airfreight or through Foreign Post office or through courier, subject to the procedure prescribed by Customs.

Disposal of Rejects/scrap/Waste/Remnants

Rejects/scrap/Waste/Remnants arising out of production process or in connection therewith may be sold in the DTA on payment of applicable duty. No duty shall be payable in case scrap/waste/remnants/rejects are destroyed within the zone after intimation to the custom authorities or destroyed outside the SEZ with the permission of Custom authorities. Destruction as stated above shall not apply to gold, silver, platinum, diamond, precious and semi-precious stones.

Management of SEZ

SEZ will be under the administrative control of the Development Commissioner.

All activities of SEZ units within the Zone, unless otherwise specified, including export and re-import of goods shall be through self certification procedure.

Samples

SEZ units may on the basis of records maintained by them, and on prior intimation to customs authorities:

- Supply or sell samples in the DTA for display/market promotion on payment of applicable duties
- Remove samples without payment of duty on furnishing a suitable undertaking to Customs authorities for bringing the goods back within a stipulated period.
- Export free samples, without any limit, including samples made in wax moulds, silver moulds and rubber moulds through all permissible mode of export including through couriers agencies/post

Entitlement for SEZ Developer

For development, operation and maintenance of infrastructure facilities in SEZs, the developer shall be eligible for the following entitlements Income tax exemption as per Section 80 IA of the Income tax Act.

Chapter-VI

6.1 IMPORT DOCUMENTATION AND PROCEDURES

Introduction:

Starting an import business is a goal of more than thousands merchants and businessman. Like an export business import business is alssso very profitable business, if an importer proceeds with the right strategies. However, the long term success and profitability of an import business greatly depends on the importer's knowledge and understanding about the international market and foreign market analysis.

Today, importing goods from abroad has becomes a big business. Everything from beverages to cars and a staggering list of other products that one might have never imagined has now become the part of the global import. Millions of products are bought, sold, represented and distributed somewhere in the world on a daily basis.

Reasons for Import

There are number of supporting reasons why import business and services is growing at such a fast rate:-

- **Availability:**

  An individual or business man or an importer needs to import because there are certain things that he can't grow or manufacture in his home country. For example Bananas in Alaska, Mahogany lumber in Maine and Ball Park franks in France.

- **Cachet:**

  A lot of things, like caviar and champagne, pack more cachet, more of an "image," if they're imported rather than home-grown. Think Scandinavian furniture, German, Germen beer, French perfume, Egyptian cotton. It all seems classier when it comes from distant place.

- **Price:**

    Price factor is also an important reason for import of products. Some products are cheaper when imported from foreign country. For example: Korean toys. Taiwanese electronics and Mexican clothing, to rattle off a few, can often be manufactured or assembled in foreign factories for far less money than if they were made on the domestic country.

    Importing goods from abroad has becomes a big business. Everything from beverages to cars--and a staggering list of other products that one might have never imagined has now become the part of the global import. Millions of products are bought, sold, represented and distributed somewhere in the world on a daily basis.

Import in India

The rising middle income groups of consumers in India and their increasing levels on expenditure on various products has resulted a faster rising demand of the Indian import business. Major imports of India include cereals, edible oils, machineries, fertilizers and petroleum products. Total import from India estimated to be around US$187.9 billion. India is also a bulk importer of edible oil, sugar, pulp and paper, newsprint, crude rubber and Iron and steel.

Import Regulatory Body

In India, all the activities related to import are handled by the Directorate General of Foreign Trade (DGFT), a government organization that also controls the export business in India. DGFT and all its regional offices work under the Ministry Commerce and Industries, Department of Commerce, Government of India. All the procedure and policies in matter related to the import is announced by the DGFT through its notification, appendices and forms.

6.2 IMPORT PROCEDURES

Starting an import business needs a proper guidelines and understanding of the foreign market. Before starting an import, it is also important for an importer to obtain all the necessary information in matters associated with foreign trade agreement. Starting an import is not a get-rich-quick-scheme. Like an export, import also requires a lot of preparations.

Preliminaries for starting Import Business

* Selecting the Commodity Market
* Proper selection of the commodity market is an important factor before starting an import.
* Commodity market data and information collected during research helps to prepare the commodity market report.
* The right market can be selected by answering the following the following questions.
* Is the product(s) an importer need to conducting his business available domestically?
* Is there a lucrative and untapped domestic market for an imported product?
* Does importing a product increase competitiveness as a business?

An importer should only proceed; if he is determined that importing certain goods will definitely make his business profitable.

Once the importer is confirmed about his importing decision, then he should proceed towards the development of the proper import business plan. While making the import plan, importer of India must evaluate the various government policies and guidelines including the rules and regulation as mentioned in the Foreign Trade Policy Procedures, 2004-09.

An importer is always free to import goods in India provided that such goods are imported under the regulations of ITC- HS Classifications of Export Import items. ITC-HS codes are divided into two schedules. All the rules and regulations related to the Indian import is mentioned in the Schedule I of the ITC.

Prohibited goods and items are not at all allowed to import while restricted items are only allowed to import though a special license issued by the Ministry of Commerce, Government of India.

State Trading Corporation of India

There are certain goods that can be only imported outside the country through a recognize agency. State Trading Corporation of India is also one of them that import a number of essential commodities to cover the domestic shortfalls and hold the price line. STC serves the national objective by arranging timely imports at most competitive prices. In the process, the Corporation makes best use of its strength in handling bulk imports, vast infrastructure and above all an experience of over four decades in fulfilling the needs of the industry. The STC is responsible for the import of goods such as bullion, vanaspati and edible oils, pulses, hydro-carbons, metals and minerals and fertilizers.

Registration of importer

Registration of importer is a pre-requisite for import of goods. The Customs will not allow clearance of goods unless the importer has obtained IEC Number from issuing authority. In India, IEC number or Importers Exporters Code is issued by the DGFT.

However, no such import business registration is necessary for persons importing goods from Nepal or Myanmar through Indo-Myanmar border or from china, through Gunji, Namgaya, shipkila or Nathula ports provided that the Value of a single Consignment does not exceed Rs. 25000/-.

Application for IEC Number:

An application for grant of IEC Code Number should be made in the prescribed Performa given at Appendix 3.I. The application duly signed by the applicant should be supported by the following documents:

1. Bank Receipt (in duplicate) / Indian demand draft for payment of the fee of Rs.1000/- Certificate from the Banker of the applicant firm as per Annexure 1 to the form.

2. Two copies of passport size photographs of the applicant duly attested by the banker of the applicant.

3. A copy of Permanent Account Number issued by Income Tax Authorities, if PAN has not been allotted, a copy of the letter of legal authority may be furnished.

4. Declaration by the applicant that the proprietors/partners/ directors of the applicant firm/company, as the case may be, are not associated as proprietor/partners/directors with any other firm/company the IEC No. is allotted with a condition that be can export only with the prior approval of the RBI India.

Process of Online Application

On-line form has been designed to ensure feeding of all the required information by prompting user wherever a field is left blank. Application has to submit scanned copies of PAN (Permanent Account Number) and bank certificate of deposits along with their application.

There are 2 options for payment of fee.

1. Demand Draft:

If fee is paid by Demand Draft, IEC will be generated only after receipt of the physical copy of the application.

2. Electronic Fund Transfer:

If IEC application fee is paid through Electronic Fund Transfer facility, IEC number will be generated by the licensing office automatically and the number can be viewed online by the applicant.

Guidelines for filling up IEC Form

1. All applications must be made in the prescribed form in duplicate, duly accompanied by Bank Receipt/ Demand Draft evidencing payment of fee.

2. Application form should be submitted in neatly typed bold letters. Handwritten forms are also accepted.

3. Each page of the document must have the signature of the authorized person with an ink pen.

4. Supporting documents in duplicate, duly self attested as specified earlier in this chapter must be enclosed wherever applicable.

5. Items of information relevant to applicant should only be filled in and remaining items may be marked 'Not Applicable'.

6. Two copies of the passport size photograph of the applicant duly attested by the applicant's banker shall be submitted.

7. Modifications of particulars of the applicant should also be furnished on this form by filling the relevant items.

Duplicate Copy of IEC No.

Duplicate copy of IEC Number is issued to those importer (or exporter) who has lost their original IEC number. Importers are required to submit an affidavit and a fee of Rs.200 to obtain a duplicate copy of IEC Number.

Surrender of IEC No.

Any importer who doesn't want to continue his import business may surrender the IEC number to the issuing authority. On receipt of such intimation, the issuing authority shall immediately cancel the same and electronically transmit it to DGFT for onward transmission to the Customs and Regional Authorities.

Guidelines and Rules for Import

The various rules and guidelines in respect of various commodities and category of importers are mentioned in the following publications issued by the Ministry of Commerce, Government of India and revised from time to time:

- Import - Export Policy, 1997-2002 as modified up to 31.03.1999
- Handbook of Procedure
- Standard Input - Output Norms, 1997-2002.
- ITC (HS) Classification of Import and Export Items.

Export- Import Policy (1997-2002)

Export Import Policy or better known as Exim Policy is a set of guidelines and instructions related to the import and export of goods. The Government of India notifies the Exim Policy for a period of five years (1997-2002) under Section 5 of the Foreign Trade (Development and Regulation Act), 1992. The current policy covers the period 2002-2007. The Export Import Policy is updated every year on the 31st of March and the modifications, improvements and new schemes became effective from 1st April of every year. All types of changes or modifications related to the Exim Policy is normally announced by the Union Minister of Commerce and Industry who co-ordinates with the Ministry of Finance, the Directorate General of Foreign Trade and its network of regional offices.

Canalization is an important feature of Exim Policy under which certain goods can be imported only by designated agencies. For an example, canalized import items like gold, in bulk, can be imported only by specified banks like SBI (State Bank of India) and some foreign banks or designated agencies.

Handbook of Procedure

Handbook of Procedure (Volume I and Volume II), which is issued by the Director General of Foreign Trade (DGFT), is a book that contains all the necessary information about the rules and regulation in the matter related to Foreign Trade Policy. Handbook of Procedure is issued at the gap of every five year with change in the Foreign Trade Policy. Between the five years terms, any further changes or modifications in the Handbook of Procedure are carried out by notifications and amendments.

Standard Input Output Norms or SION

Standard Input Output Norms or SION in short is standard norms which define the amount of input/inputs required to manufacture a unit of output for export purpose. Input output norms are applicable for the products such as electronics, engineering, chemical, food products including fish and marine products, handicraft, plastic and leather products etc. An application for modification of existing Standard Input-Output norms may be filed by manufacturer exporter and merchant-exporter.

The Directorate General of Foreign Trade (DGFT) from time to time issue notifications for fixation or addition of SION for different export products. Fixation of Standard Input Output Norms facilitates issues of Advance License to the exporters of the items without any need for referring the same to the Headquarter office of DGFT on repeat basis.

ITC- HS Codes

ITC- HS codes or better known as Indian Trade Clarification based on Harmonized System of Coding was adopted in India for import-export business. Indian custom uses an eight digit ITC HS Codes to suit the international trade requirements.

Harmonized System codes are divided into two schedules. Schedule I describe the rules and guidelines related to import policies where as Schedule II describe the rules and regulation related to export policies.

Schedule I of the ITC-HS code is divided into 21 sections and each section is further divided into chapters. The total number of chapters in the schedule I is 98. The chapters are further divided into sub-heading under which different HS codes are mentioned. Schedule II of the ITC-HS code contain 97 chapters giving all the details about the guidelines related to the export policies.

Selecting the Overseas exporter

Selecting an overseas exporter raises a number of issues for the importer such as language differences, payment methods and increased paperwork requirements. However, with a little research and proper planning these challenges can be easily overcome. In this chapter, we will discuss the various factors required for consideration of an overseas exporter or supplier and the methods for selecting overseas suppliers.

Legal considerations

Trading with overseas supplier is quite different from trading in India, particularly when dealing with a country outside Asia, so an importer should consider the following factor before import.

- Whether there is import or restricted trade at either end of the transaction.

- Whether technical standards in supplier's country meet Indian requirements.

- Who is liable if a product causes harm or loss?

- Whether imported goods infringe any intellectual property rights or not.

- Who bears insurance costs at each stage of transit?

- A well-drafted written contract will help to avoid disagreements or disputes.

Other considerations

There is a range of other factors that an importer should bear in mind:

- Language differences are important. It's not just a matter of communication - make sure any labeling or other printed materials are error-free.

- Payment methods for international trade transactions are an import issue for import. So, importer must take a proper care while selected a payment methods such as Letter of Credit (Documentary Credit, or Lc), Documentary Collection, Advance Payment Receipt.

- Shipping of goods is also a complicated process. Given the increased distances and the need to cross borders.

- Understanding the business and social practices of supplier's country can help build trust and develop relationships.

- The origin of your goods can affect the level of duty you pay. Some goods attract a preferential rate of duty, so you need to check where your supplier's raw materials have come from. Visiting suppliers is the best way of doing this.

Capability of Overseas Supplier

Successful completion of an import transaction mainly depends upon the capability of the overseas supplier to fulfill that contact. Therefore, it becomes important for the importer to properly verify the foreign exporter before entering into a contract with the exporter. Confidential information about the exporter may obtain through the banks and Indian embassies abroad. The importer can also take the assistance of Credit Information Agencies for specific commercial information on overseas suppliers.

Sources of Information

The information regarding overseas exporter and suppliers can generally be obtained from the following sources:

- Trade Directories and Yellow pages, like Singapore yellow pages, Japan yellow pages, USA yellow pages etc. available from leading booksellers in India.

- Consulate Generals and Trade Representative of various countries in India and abroad.

- Friends and relatives in foreign countries.

- International Trade Fairs and Exhibitions for which International Trade Promotions Organization (ITPO), Pragati Madian, New Delhi, can be contacted.

- Chambers of Commerce as per addresses.

- Directorates of Industries, etc.

- Indenting Agent of Foreign Suppliers.

- Visiting popular Web-sites.

Role of Overseas Agents in India

Some overseas suppliers have appointed their agents in India. These agents procure orders from the Indian parties and arrange for the supply

204 Export and Import

of goods from abroad. It is advisable to import through such agents as they can be readily contacted in case of any difficulty with regards to quality of goods, payment and documentation.

Finalizing the Terms of Import

Once importer is satisfied with the sample and the creditworthiness of the overseas exporter, importer can proceed further to finalization the terms of the import contract. Import's contract need to be carefully and comprehensively drafted incorporating there in precise terms, all relevant conditions of the trade deal. There should not be any ambiguity regarding the exact specifications of the goods and terms of the purchase including import price, mode of payment, type of packaging, port of shipment, delivery schedule, replacement of defective goods supplied, after sale services/warranty coverage etc.

Import License

While the majority of the goods are freely importable, the Exim Policy (2007) of India prohibits import of certain categories of products as well as conditional import of certain items. In such a situation it becomes important for the importer to have an import license issued by the issuing authorities of the Government of India.

Import License Issuing Authority

In India, Import License is issued by the Director General of Foreign Trade. DGFT Delhi office is situated in Udyog Bhawan, New Delhi 110011.

Validity of Import License

Import Licenses are valid for 24 months for capital goods and 18 months for raw materials components, consumable and spares, with the license term renewable.

Sample of Import License

A typical sample of import license consists of two copies-

Foreign Exchange Control Copy:

> To be utilized for effecting remittance to foreign seller or for opening letter of credit

Customs Copy:

To be utilized for presenting to Customs authority enabling them to clear the goods. In the absence of custom copy, import will be declared as an unauthorized import, liable for confiscation and or penalty.

6.3 CATEGORIES OF IMPORT

All types of imported goods come under the following four categories:

* **Freely importable items:**

    Most capital goods fall into this category. Any product declared as Freely Importable Item does not require import licenses.

* **Licensed Imports:**

    There are number of goods, which can only be importer under an import license. This category includes several broad product groups that are classified as consumer goods; precious and semi-precious stones; products related to safety and security; seeds, plants and animals; some insecticides, pharmaceuticals and chemicals; some electronically items; several items reserved for production by the small-scale sector; and 17 miscellaneous or special-category items.

* **Canalised Items:**

    There are certain canalised items that can only be importer in India through specified channels or government agencies. These include petroleum products (to be imported only by the Indian Oil Corporation); nitrogenous phosphatic, potassic and complex chemical fertilizers (by the Minerals and Metals Trading Corporation) vitamin- A drugs (by the State Trading Corporation); oils and seeds (by the State Trading Corporation and Hindustan Vegetable Oils); and cereals (by the Food Corporation of India).

* **Prohibited items:**

    Only four items-tallow fat, animal rennet, wild animals and unprocessed ivory-are completely banned from importation.

Category of Importer

On the basis of product to be imported and its target buyer, importers categories are divided into three groups for the purpose of obtaining import licensing:

1.   Actual Users- An actual user applies for and receives a license to import of any item for personal use rather than for business or trade purpose.

2.   Registered exporters defined as those who have a valid registration certificate issued by an export promotion council, commodity board or other registered authority designated by the Government for purposes of export-promotion.

3.   Others.

The two types of actual user license are:

1.   **General Licenses :**

This license can be used for the imports of goods from all countries, except those countries from which imports are prohibited;

2.   **Specific Licenses:**

This license can only be used for imports from a specific country.

Custom Inspection

Any violation in the import license is usually scanned by the custom officials of the custom department. Customer inspector and other custom officials have authority to inspect and evaluate the goods to be imported. It's a part of their job to determine whether imports conform to the description in the import License or not. Custom official even have right to charge fines and penalties if any violation in the import license is found to be done by the importer.

Import trade governing bodies

Import in India is governed by the certain rules and regulation, which are issued by the import-export governing bodies. Import Export government authorities decide which items will be imported and which item will be prohibited. The quantity of goods to be imported and tax imposed on the imported goods is also under the control of import governing body. Import-Export governing bodies also play an important role in settling the Foreign Trade Agreement in matters related to import of goods.

Ministry of Commerce and Industry

The Ministry of Commerce and Industry is the nodal authority for formulating and implementing the foreign trade policy in matter related to Import. The Department of Commerce play a key role in matters related to multilateral and bilateral commercial relations, state trading, export promotion measures and development and regulation of certain import oriented industries and commodities.

There are two departments under the Ministry of Commerce and Industry. The first one is the Department of Commerce and the second is Department of Industrial Policy & Promotion. The department of Ministry of Commerce which is sometimes also termed as Department of Industrial Policy & Promotion was established in the year 1995, and in the year 2000 Department of Industrial Development was merged with it.

Ministry of Commerce and Industry has its offices in all the major cities. Its Delhi office is located at Udyog Bhavan, New Delhi – 110011 India

Directorate General of Foreign Trade (DGFT)

DGFT or Directorate General of Foreign Trade is a government organization in India responsible for the formulation of guidelines and principles for importers as well as exporters of country.

Preparation, formulation and implication of Exim Policies are one of the main functions of DGFT. Apart from Exim Policy, DGFT is also responsible for issuing IEC or Import Export Code. IEC codes are mandatory for carrying out import export trade operations and enable companies to acquire benefits on their imports/exports, customs, exports promotion council etc in India. DGFT also play an important role in controlling DEPB rates and setting standard input-output norms. Any changes or formulation or addition of new codes in ITC-HS Codes are also carried out by DGFT (Directorate General of Foreign Trade).

DGFT has its offices in all the major cities. Its Delhi office is located at IP Bhawan, New Delhi.

6.4   CENTRAL BOARD OF EXCISES CUSTOMS (CBEC)

The Central Board of Excises Customs (CBEC) under Ministry of Finance is the controlling authority to handle custom duty related matters. CBEC regularly publishes the "Indian Customs Tariff Guide that provides all types of information on custom duty rules and regulation in India.

Custom duty not only raises money for the Central Government but also helps the government to prevent the illegal imports and exports of goods from India. The Central government has emergency powers to increase import or export duties whenever necessary after a notification in the session of Parliament.

Objectives of Custom Duties

- Regulating the amount of import in India in order to protect the domestic market.
- Protecting Indian Industry from undue competition
- Prohibiting certain imports of goods for achieving the policy objectives of the Government.
- Regulating imports
- Coordinating legal provisions with other laws dealing with foreign exchange such as Foreign Trade Act, Foreign Exchange Regulation Act, Conservation of Foreign Exchange and Prevention of Smuggling Act, etc.

All import goods are classified into categories known as called "headings" and "subheadings" (Harmonised System Codes) for the purpose of levy of duty. For each sub-heading, a specific rate of duty has been prescribed in the Customs Tariff Act, 1975.

Import of Samples

Before making a confirmed order, it is important for the importer to ask for a sample of the original manufactured product that can be shown or demonstrated for Customer appreciation and familiarization. Import of samples help the importer to deciding the total quantity of product need to be imported as well as also allows importer to make any necessary changes in the final product.

Import samples

The import samples are basically specimens of the product, which is finally given to the importer. It may include consumer goods, consumer durables, prototypes of engineering goods or even high value equipment, machineries (including agricultural machinery) and their accessories. Import of samples can be done by the trade, industry, individuals, Companies, Associations, Research Institutes or Laboratories. These can also be brought by the Representatives of foreign Manufacturer as a part of their personal Baggage or through port or in Courier. They can also be sent by Manufacturers/Traders abroad to above parties in India.

Geneva Convention, 1952

Import of samples of goods is exempt from import duties under Geneva Convention of 7th November, 1952. India is also a signatory to a 1952 convention to facilitate the Importation of Commercial samples and Advertising materials. The notifications issued in this regard enable duty free import of genuine Commercial samples into the country for smooth flow of trade.

Restriction on Import of Samples

However, goods which are prohibited under Foreign Trade (Development and Regulation) Act, 1992 are not allowed to be imported as samples e.g. wild animals, wild birds and parts of wild animals and birds, ivory, arms & ammunitions, and Narcotic drugs.

Value limit

The bonafide trade samples can be imported by trade and industry provided the said goods have been supplied free of charge. For duty free clearance the value of individual sample should not exceed Rs.5000/- and aggregate value should not exceed Rs.60, 000/- per year or 15 units of samples in a year. This strategy avoids the risk of not paying Customs Duty through repeated imports of samples in smaller lots.

Machinery import

Import of machinery products, which are prototypes of engineering goods can also be imported duty free if the value does not exceed Rs.10000/-.

In case the value of machinery exceeds more than Rs.10000/- then such goods are always chargeable to duty.

Privacy of Import Samples

In case of high valued machinery the importer can import a sample under privacy. On the request of importer, the Customs authority may also seal the machinery during its journey from the port of importation to the place of demonstration and it is unsealed only at the place of operation or place of demonstration.

Failure to re-export

In case of any damage to the previously send import sample of product, the same sample can be send again within the time period of 9 months. However, the Assistant Commissioner of Customs may under special circumstances extend the period of 9 months for a further reasonable period.

Import Duties

The concept of import duty is very wide and is almost applicable to every product or item imported to India barring a few goods like food grains, fertilizer, life saving drugs and equipment etc. Import duties form a significant source of revenue for the country and are levied on the goods and at the rates specified in the Schedules to the Customs Tariff Act, 1975.

Import through Sea

Territorial water extends up to 12 nautical miles into the sea from the coast of India and so the liability to pay import duty commences as soon as goods enter the territorial waters of India. No duty is livable on goods which are in transit in the same ship or if goods are in transit from one ship to another.

Basic duty

Basic Duty is a type of duty or tax imposed under the Customs Act (1962). Basic Customs Duty varies for different items from 5% to 40%. The duty rates are mentioned in the First Schedule of the Customs Tariff Act, 1975 and have been amended from time to time under the Finance Act. The duty may be fixed on ad –valorem basis or specific rate basis. The Central Government has the power to reduce or exempt any good from these duties.

Additional customs

Additional duty also known as countervailing duty or C.V.D is equal to excise duty imposed on a like product manufactured or produced in India. It is implemented under the Section 3 (1) of the Indian Custom Tariff Act. The Government has exempted all goods, when imported into India for subsequent sale, from the whole of the additional duty of customs leviable thereon under Sub-Section (5) of Section 3 of the Customs Tariff Act vide Customs Tariff Notification No. 102/2007 dated 14th September 2007. However, the importers will be first required to pay the said duty and thereafter required to claim the refund.

Special additional duty

Special Additional Duty of Customs is imposed at the rate of 4% in order to provide a level playing field to indigenous goods which have to bear sales tax. This duty is to computed on the aggregate of –

- assessable value;
- basic duty of Customs;
- surcharge; and
- additional duty of Customs leviable under section 3 of the Customs Tariff Act, 1975 (c.v.d.)

Anti-Dumping Duty

Dumping means exporting goods in a foreign market at a price which is less than their cost of production or below their "fair" market value. Dumping gives a hard competition to a domestic goods manufacturer. So, to counteract this dumping, the Indian government has formulated certain guidelines and policies. Imposing duty on imported goods is also one of them and is known as Anti-Dumping Duty.

All the laws related to anti-dumping duties are mention in the sections 9A, 9B and 9C of the Indian Customs Tariff Act (1975), and the Indian Customs Tariff Rules (1995). These laws are based on the Agreement on Anti-Dumping which is in pursuance of Article VI of GATT 1994.

The concept of import duty is very wide and is almost applicable to every product or item imported to India barring a few goods like food grains, fertilizer, life saving drugs and equipment etc. Import duties form a significant source of revenue for the country and are levied on the goods and at the rates specified in the Schedules to the Customs Tariff Act, 1975.

Import through Sea

Territorial water extends up to 12 nautical miles into the sea from the coast of India and so the liability to pay import duty commences as soon as goods enter the territorial waters of India. No duty is livable on goods which are in transit in the same ship or if goods are in transit from one ship to another.

Basic duty

Basic Duty is a type of duty or tax imposed under the Customs Act (1962). Basic Customs Duty varies for different items from 5% to 40%. The duty rates are mentioned in the First Schedule of the Customs Tariff Act, 1975 and have been amended from time to time under the Finance Act. The duty may be fixed on ad –valorem basis or specific rate basis. The Central Government has the power to reduce or exempt any good from these duties.

Additional customs

Additional duty also known as countervailing duty or C.V.D is equal to excise duty imposed on a like product manufactured or produced in India. It is implemented under the Section 3 (1) of the Indian Custom Tariff Act. The Government has exempted all goods, when imported into India for subsequent sale, from the whole of the additional duty of customs leviable thereon under Sub-Section (5) of Section 3 of the Customs Tariff Act vide Customs Tariff Notification No. 102/2007 dated 14th September 2007. However, the importers will be first required to pay the said duty and thereafter required to claim the refund.

6.5   IMPORT RISKS

Like an export, import of goods is also associated with various types of risks. Some of these are

- Transport Risk – This risk is associated with the loss of goods during transportation.
- Quality Risk – This risk is associated with the final quality of the products.

- Delivery Risk – This risk arises when the goods are not delivered on time.

- Exchange Risk – This risk arises due to the change in the value of currency.

These risks are explained more fully below.

Transport Risk

For a better transport risk management, an importer must ensure that the goods supplied by the exporter is insured. Whether the goods are transported by Sea or by Air, the risk can be covered by Insurance. It is always advisable to set out the agreement between the parties as to the type of cover to be obtained in the Contract of Sale. Often Importers will wish to obtain Insurance cover from their own Insurance Company under a 'blanket cover' called an 'Open Policy' thus taking advantage of bulk billing and other relationships.

Quality risk

The proper quality risk analysis is important for the importer to ensure that the final products are as good as the sample. Occasionally, it has been found that the goods are not in accordance with samples, quality is not as specified, or they are otherwise unsatisfactory. To handle such situations in future, importer must take necessary protective measures in advance. One the best method to avoid such situation is to investigate the reputation and standing of the supplier. Even before receiving the final product, inspection can be done from the importer side or exporter side or by a third party agency.

In case of Bill of Exchange, with documents released against acceptance, the Importer is able to inspect the goods before payment is made to the Supplier at the maturity date. In this method of payment, if the goods are not in accordance with the Contract of Sale the Importer is able to stop payment on the accepted draft prior to maturity. Importers should consider what measures can be taken to ensure that the need for legal action does not arise. If the Importer has an agent in the Supplier's country it may be possible for closer supervision to be maintained over shipments.

Delivery Risk

Delivery of goods on time is important factor for the importer to reach the target market. For example any product or item which has been ordered for Christmas is of no use if it is received after the Christmas. Importer must make the import contract very specific, so that importer always has an option of refusing payment if it is apparent that goods have not been shipped by the specific shipment date. Where an Importer is paying for goods by means of a Documentary Credit, the Issuing Bank can be instructed to include a 'latest date for shipment' in the terms of the Credit.

Exchange Risk

Before entering into a commercial contract, it is always advisable for the importer to determine the value of the product in domestic currency. As there is always a gap between the time of entering into the contract and the actual payment for the goods is received, so determining the value of the good in domestic currency will help an exporter to quote the right price for the product.

- Contracting to import in Indian Rupees.
- Entering into a Foreign Exchange Contract through Bank.
- Offsetting Export receivables against Import payables in the same currency by using a Foreign Currency Account.
- Where Pre / Post-Shipment Finance is provided with a Foreign Currency Loan in the currency of the transaction and Export receipts repay the loan.

6.6   IMPORT INCENTIVES UNDER SPECIAL SCHEMES

The Government of India offers many incentives to Indian importer under special schemes. These schemes are mostly available on those imported product, which will be latter on used for manufacturing of goods meant for export. This not only stimulates the industrial growth and development but also brings the foreign currency after the final export process. The following are some of the important import incentives offered by the Government of India, which significantly reduce the effective tax rates for the import companies.

Preferential Rates

Any type of import incentive under preferential rate is only applicable for the import o goods from certain preferential countries such as Mauritius, Seychelles and Tonga provided certain conditions are satisfied. The certificate of origin is very important in order to avail of the benefits of such concessional rates of duty.

DEPB

Duty Entitlement Pass Book in short DEPB is basically an export incentive scheme. The objective of DEPB scheme is to neutralize the incidence of basic custom duty on the import content of the exported products. Notified on 1/4/1997, the DEPB Scheme consisted of (a) Post-export DEPB and (b) Pre-export DEPB. The pre-export DEPB scheme was abolished w.e.f. 1/4/2000. Under the post-export DEPB, which is issued after exports, the exporter is given a Duty Entitlement Pass Book at a pre-determined credit on the FOB value. The DEPB allows import of any items except the items which are otherwise restricted for imports.

Duty Drawback

Duty Drawback rates in India is the special rebate given under the Section 75 of Indian Customs Act on exported products or materials. Duty drawback rates or concession are only applicable on products which are used in the processing of goods manufactured in India and then exported to foreign countries. Duty Drawback is not given on inputs obtained without payment of customs or excise duty. In case of re-export of goods, it should be done within 2 years from the date of payment of duty when they were imported. 98% of the duty is allowable as drawback, only after inspection. If the goods imported are used before its re-export, the drawback will be allowed as at reduced per cent.

All industry drawback rates are fixed by Directorate of Drawback, Dept. of Revenue, Ministry of Finance and Government of India and are periodically revised - normally on 1st June every year. Section 37 of Central Excise Act allows Central Government to frame rules for purpose of the Act. Under these powers, 'Customs and Central Excise Duties Drawback Rules, 1995' have been framed.

DFRC

Under the Duty Free Replenishment Certificate (DFRC) schemes, import incentives are given to the exporter for the import of inputs used in the manufacture of goods without payment of basic customs duty. Such inputs shall be subject to the payment of additional customs duty equal to the excise duty at the time of import. Duty Free Replenishment Certificate (DFRC) shall be available for exports only up to 30.04.2006 and from 01.05.2006 this scheme is being replaced by the Duty Free Import Authorisation (DFIA).

DFIA

Effective from 1st May, 2006, Duty Free Import Authorisation or DFIA in short is issued to allow duty free import of inputs which are used in the manufacture of the export product (making normal allowance for wastage), and fuel, energy, catalyst etc. which are consumed or utilised in the course of their use to obtain the export product. Duty Free Import Authorisation is issued on the basis of inputs and export items given under Standard Input and Output Norms (SION).

Deemed Exports

Deemed Export is a special type of transaction in which the payment is received before the goods are delivered. The payment can be done in Indian Rupees or in Foreign Exchange. As the deemed export is also a source of foreign exchange, so the Government of India has given the benefit duty free import of inputs.

Agri Export Zones

Various importers that come under the Agri Export Zones are entitled to all the import facilities and incentives.

Served from India

In order to create a powerful "Served from India" brand all over the world, the government has provided different type of import incentive to the invisible export providers. Under the Served from India Scheme, import incentive is given for import of any capital goods, spares, office equipment and professional equipment.

Manufacture under Bond

Under the Manufacture under Bond Scheme, all factories registered to produce their goods for export are exempted from import duty and other taxes on inputs used to manufacture such goods. Against this the manufacturer is allowed to import goods without paying any customs duty. The production is made under the supervision of customs or excise authority.

Export Promotion Capital Goods Scheme (EPCG)

EPCG is a special type of incentive given to the EPCG license holder. Capital goods imported under EPCG Scheme are subject to actual user condition and the same cannot be transferred /sold till the fulfillment of export obligation specified in the license. In order to ensure that the capital goods imported under EPCG Scheme, the license holder is required to produce certificate from the jurisdictional Central Excise Authority (CEA) or Chartered Engineer (CE) confirming installation of such capital goods in the declared premises. Under Export Promotion Capital Goods (EPCG) scheme, a license holder can import capital goods such as plant, machinery, equipment, components and spare parts of the machinery at concessional rate of customs duty of 5% and without CVD and special duty.

6.7 METHODS OF PAYMENT IN IMPORT TRADE

There is no predefined definition of personal import. In general a personal import is a direct purchase of foreign goods from overseas mail order companies, retailers, manufacturers or by an individual for the purpose of personal use.

The most common terms of purchase are as follows:

- Consignment Purchase
- Cash-in-Advance (Pre-Payment)
- Down Payment
- Open Account
- Documentary Collections
- Letters of Credit

Consignment Purchase

Consignment purchase terms can be the most beneficial method of payment for the importer. In this method of purchase, importer makes the payment only once the goods or imported items are sold to the end user. In case of no selling, the same item is returned to the foreign supplier. Consignment purchase is considered the most risky and time taking method of payment for the exporter.

Cash-in-Advance (Pre-Payment)

Cash in Advance is a pre-payment method in which, an importer the payment for the items to be imported in advance prior to the shipment of goods. The importer must trust that the supplier will ship the product on time and that the goods will be as advertised. Cash-in-Advance method of payment creates a lot of risk factors for the importers. However, this method of payment is inexpensive as it involves direct importer-exporter contact without commercial bank involvement.

In international trade, Cash in Advance methods of payment is usually done when-

- The Importer has not been long established.
- The Importer's credit status is doubtful or unsatisfactory.
- The country or political risks are very high in the importer's country.
- The product is in heavy demand and the seller does not have to accommodate an Importer's financing request in order to sell the merchandise.

Down Payment

In the method of down payment, an importer pays a fraction of the total amount of the items to be imported in advance. The down payment methods have both advantages and disadvantages. The advantage is that it induces the exporter or seller to begin performance without the importer or buyer paying the full agreed price in advance and the disadvantage is that there is a possibility the Seller or exporter may never deliver the goods even though it has the Buyer's down payment.

Open Account

In case of an open account, an importer takes the delivery of good and ensures the supplier to make the payment at some specific date in the future. Importer is also not required to issue any negotiable instrument evidencing his legal commitment to pay at the appointed time. This type of payment methods are mostly seen where when the importer/buyer has a strong credit history and is well-known to the seller. Open Account method of payment offers no protection in case of non-payment to the seller.

There are many merits and demerits of open account terms. Under an open account payment method, title to the goods usually passes from the seller to the buyer prior to payment and subjects the seller to risk of default by the Buyer. Furthermore, there may be a time delay in payment, depending on how quickly documents are exchanged between Seller and Buyer. While this payment term involves the fewest restrictions and the lowest cost for the Buyer, it also presents the Seller with the highest degree of payment risk and is employed only between a Buyer and a Seller who have a long-term relationship involving a great level of mutual trust.

Documentary Collections

Documentary Collection is an important bank payment method under, which the sale transaction is settled by the bank through an exchange of documents. In this process the seller's instructs his bank to forwards documents related to the export of goods to the buyer's bank with a request to present these documents to the buyer for payment, indicating when and on what conditions these documents can be released to the buyer.

The buyer may obtain possession of goods and clear them through customs, if the buyer has the shipping documents such as original bill of lading, certificate of origin, etc. However, the documents are only given to the buyer after payment has been made ("Documents against Payment") or payment undertaking has been given - the buyer has accepted a bill of exchange issued by the seller and payable at a certain date in the future (maturity date) ("Documents against Acceptance").

Documentary Collections make easy import-export operations within low cost. But it does not provide same level of protection as the letter of credit as it does not involve any kind of bank guarantee like letter of credit.

Letter of Credit

A letter of credit is the most well known method of payment in international trade. Under an import letter of credit, importer's bank guarantees to the supplier that the bank will pay mentioned amount in the agreement, once supplier or exporter meet the terms and conditions of the letter of credit. In this method of payment, plays an intermediary role to help complete the trade transaction. The bank deals only in documents and does not inspect the goods themselves. Letters of Credit are issued subject to the Uniforms Customs & Practice for Documentary Credits (UCPDC)(UCP). This set of rules is produced by the International Chamber of Commerce and Industries (CII).

Documents against Acceptance:

Instructions given by an exporter to a bank that the documents attached to the draft for collection are deliverable to the drawee only against his or her acceptance of the draft.

6.8 CUSTOMS CLEARANCE OF IMPORTED GOODS

All goods imported into India have to pass through the procedure of customs for proper examination, appraisal, assessment and evaluation. This helps the custom authorities to charge the proper tax and also check the goods against the illegal import. Also it is important to note that no import is allowed in India if the importer doesn't have the IEC number issued by the DFGT. There is no requirement of IEC number if the goods are imported for the personal use.

Bill of Entry

A Bill of Entry also known as Shipment Bill is a statement of the nature and value of goods to be imported or exported, prepared by the shipper and presented to a customhouse. The importer clearing the goods for domestic consumption has to file bill of entry in four copies; original and duplicate are meant for customs, third copy for the importer and the fourth copy is meant for the bank for making remittances.

If the goods are cleared through the EDI system, no formal Bill of Entry is filed as it is generated in the computer system, but the importer is required to file a cargo declaration having prescribed particulars required for processing of the entry for customs clearance.

In the non-EDI system along with the bill of entry filed by the importer or his representative the following documents are also generally required:-

- Signed invoice
- Packing list
- Bill of Lading or Delivery Order/Airway Bill
- GATT declaration form duly filled in
- Importers/ CHA's declaration
- License wherever necessary
- Letter of Credit/Bank Draft/wherever necessary
- Insurance document
- Import license
- Industrial License, if required
- Test report in case of chemicals
- Adhoc exemption order
- DEEC Book/DEPB in original
- Catalogue, Technical write up, Literature in case of machineries, spares or chemicals as may be applicable
- Separately split up value of spares, components machineries
- Certificate of Origin, if preferential rate of duty is claimed
- No Commission declaration

Amendment of Bill of Entry

Whenever mistakes are noticed after submission of documents, amendments to the bill of entry is carried out with the approval of Deputy/Assistant Commissioner.

Green Channel facility

Some major importers have been given the green channel clearance facility. It means clearance of goods is done without routine examination of the goods. They have to make a declaration in the declaration form at the time of filing of bill of entry. The appraisement is done as per normal procedure except that there would be no physical examination of the goods.

Payment of Duty

Import duty may be paid in the designated banks or through TR-6 challans. Different Custom Houses have authorized different banks for payment of duty and is necessary to check the name of the bank and the branch before depositing the duty.

Prior Entry for Shipping Bill or Bill of Entry

For faster clearance of the goods, provision has been made in section 46 of the Act, to allow filing of bill of entry prior to arrival of goods. This bill of entry is valid if vessel/aircraft carrying the goods arrive within 30 days from the date of presentation of bill of entry.

Specialized Schemes

Import of goods under specialized scheme such as DEEC and EOU etc is required to execute bonds with the custom authorities. In case failure of bond, importer is required to pay the duty livable on those goods. The amount of bond would be equal to the amount of duty livable on the imported goods. The bank guarantee is also required along with the bond. However, the amount of bank guarantee depends upon the status of the importer like Super Star Trading House/Trading House etc.

Bill of Entry for Bond/Warehousing

A separate form of bill of entry is used for clearance of goods for warehousing. Assessment of this bill of entry is done in the same manner as the normal bill of entry and then the duty payable is determined.

www.ingramcontent.com/pod-product-compliance
Lightning Source LLC
Chambersburg PA
CBHW021923190326
41519CB00009B/892